Emily ~
always choose
a happy heart!

I AM Before "I Do"

Unsolicited Advice on LOVE & Goddess Philosophy

Ranee A. Spina

a raz book production

a raz book production
Studio City, CA 91604

Visit our website at www.iambeforeido.com

Layout, design, and illustrations by Ranee A. Spina

Printed in the United States of America
First Printing: March 2006

Think of this book

as my attempt to walk the fine line

between having respect

for your individual paths

and me exercising

some loving leadership.

Contents

Contents

Feel free to read the topics in this book
in any order that you desire.

"There are no rules, only choices."

"I wanted to find out where I was going
before I found out who was going with me."

Mariska Hargitay

Make this book your own.
Write yourself notes that pertain to
your individual situation.
Tell your girlfriends to get their own copy!

Chapter 1

A Happy Heart

THE institution of marriage: actually standing before God, a priest, rabbi, justice of the peace, or Elvis in Las Vegas, and making a vow to be part of someone else's life. You will now determine 50% of his happiness, sadness, and everything in between. He will now determine 50% of your happiness, sadness, and everything in between.

Wow, what power that is! What I do not understand is why so many women disregard that power and set themselves up for failure.

Why not give yourself a 70-80% chance for this important commitment to be successful? One of the reasons the divorce rate is so high is that people tend to set themselves up for failure. We enter into a marriage with a 20-30% chance of true success, because we fail to take stock of:

1- What we are,
2- What we have, and
3- What we want.

All the hoping, praying, and closing our eyes to the truth is not going to change the facts. You must take responsibility for the choices you make. Together, we will analyze important relationship issues, and through humor and common sense (which is not all that common), you will clearly see pitfalls to avoid in the future (if you so choose).

Give yourself the advantage now, by taking the time to consider the topics in this book. Only then will you have the peace of mind that is essential for building a healthy and truly happy union. It is your choice to be happy 360 days out of the year or just 5 days out of the year.

Here's to happy and healthy hearts 360 days out of the year!

If you have never stood upon your own feet,
it is understandable that you may feel uneasy
facing new experiences.

But, I promise you,
as you put one foot in front of the other,
you will get stronger and more confident with each step.

Chapter II
Your Worth

WHY is it that women of all ages tend to focus on what they are not, instead of what they *are*?

Discover your self-worth.

What do you bring to this world? What defines you? A man? There has to be more to you than the man in your life or the man you will marry one fine day. That is what this book is all about - focusing on what *you* are, what *you* want, and what *you* need. Then, and only then, can you know what man would be your complementary match.

Complement n. - That which adds to or fits in with something else.

I know it will be hard for some of you to look inside yourself. I also know that some of you will do *whatever* it takes to avoid taking responsibility for your choices. Humor me. For just one month, put aside all of your preconceived notions about yourself, men, and the world.

Here is an easy way to begin:
Think about what gives you a sense of, *"Wow, I did that!" (Having irresponsible, unprotected sex and getting pregnant do not count here.)* What makes your heart sing? What do you enjoy doing that brings you back to yourself and makes you feel good about who you are? You will need to remember to *always have a sense of self.* A mate WILL NOT REPLACE what gives you self-worth.

A girl I know married eight years ago at age twenty-three. She was in a BIG HURRY and gave her boyfriend an ultimatum, "Marry me or we're breaking up." *(He should have walked.)* She now confesses that she "couldn't wait to cook and clean for him." *(That gets old real fast.)* At age 31 she is asking herself, "Who am I? Yes, I'm a good mom and a good homemaker, BUT WHO AM I?"

"Wisdom to learn,
to change, to let go.
Acceptance of the truth
and beauty within yourself."

Maureen Doan

She is now trying to figure out what she should have figured out in her twenties, *before* the husband and the two children became a part of her life. She has little time to herself to discover what she is capable of, what makes her so special, and what talents she possesses. The inner turmoil she is experiencing is what she would have avoided **IF SHE WAS NOT IN SUCH A BIG HURRY TO GET MARRIED!** Will her marriage survive her self-development process? That is yet to be seen.

If you are thinking of going straight from the "security" of your parents to the "security" of a husband - forget it. How will you ever know what is important to you alone? How will you ever have the courage to face the world as a strong, confident, self-assured woman who knows she can stand on her own two feet? Become responsible for your own well-being. Live on your own, where you have the opportunity to experience being self-sufficient *with no security.* I do not care if you have to use cardboard boxes for tables and sleep on an air mattress while shacking up with some friends. You should only have to answer to your pillow. **This stage will prove to be the most important growth phase of your entire life.** If you attempt to skip this important part of your personal growth, it will come back to haunt you -- I promise you that.

Self-fulfillment and self-worth are not found in "being chosen by" or "belonging to" a boyfriend or husband. And, there is no need to rush the self-discovery process. Even you "mommy wannabes" should know that a woman is fertile well beyond the age of thirty. Once a significant other, or a child, becomes part of your life, the time that is necessary to develop your interesting, cultivated, educated, and absolutely wonderful self image diminishes.

Maybe you never gave yourself the chance to develop an interesting, cultivated, educated, and absolutely wonderful self-image, BECAUSE you have been jumping from boyfriend to boyfriend, or worse - husband to husband. *HELLO?* We tend to have the most drastic personal growth when we are single, not when we are concerned about being part of a couple.

"Use and 'abuse' your twenties."

How many times have you been nuts over some guy, only to look back later down the road and say to yourself, "What was I thinking?" *Because, of course, the "dumb-girl" syndrome hits all of us.* This syndrome messes with our common sense area of the brain. We focus on his cute face, his great biceps, his nice car, his powerful position, or the thought that someone might actually adore us. We seem to overlook all the lame, "red flag," contradictory, or disgusting characteristics that will make us sick when we revisit those memories months after the relationship has ended. But, how do we know what we want in a mate if we have not taken the time to figure out our own self-worth?

This is not a lesson on self-esteem. (There are plenty of good books to boost your self-esteem from whatever issues that may be having an impact on your psyche.) This is a lesson about YOU.

How can you say you are ready to commit yourself to someone else when you have not made any type of commitment to yourself?

Get out there and learn, experience, see, and do any and all things that are important to you alone.

Take the time to focus on all the good you bring to the world. I ask you to embrace the healthy mindset that you want nothing less than what you are: a fabulous mate for a fabulous mate.

☐ I totally get this chapter.

☐ I should re-read this chapter.

☐ __________ (fill in name) needs to read this chapter.

"I hope you never fear those mountains in the distance,
Never settle for the path of least resistance,
Living might mean taking chances,
But they're worth taking,
Loving might be a mistake,
But it's worth making.

Don't let some hell-bent heart leave you bitter,
When you come to selling out - reconsider,
Give the heavens above more than just a passing glance,

And when you get the choice to sit it out or dance,
I hope you dance . . ."

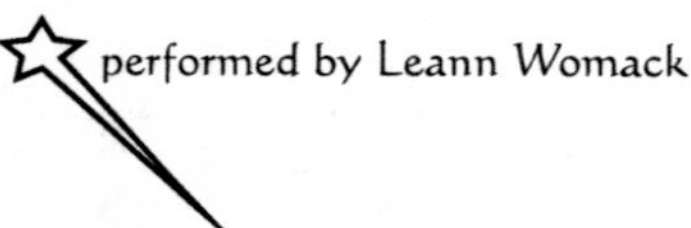

Chapter III

Get Past the Old and Familiar

HOW can we believe that it is possible to know what the man *who is going to adore us for the rest of his life* looks like?

Right now, get over your so-called "type." As of this very minute, your so-called "type" no longer exists. I have waved my magic wand over you, and you are now open to the idea that you have no idea what the man *who is going to adore you for the rest of his life* looks like.

Where does the "type" that we are initially attracted to come from? I believe it could be many factors. Maybe it is an image we grew up with, such as a father or an older brother that we were comfortable with as a child. Maybe it is the "look" of your high school crush or a celebrity that you find sexually attractive.

Yes, physical attraction is necessary, but guys will either get cuter or become repulsive as you get to know their personality traits. We all have heard of the drop dead gorgeous guy who after three dates fits the description of "jerk" instead of "gorgeous." We must keep our minds open to any and all experiences.

But, how do we do that?
We become aware of our norm. Your norm is that which you are usually attracted to when it comes to men. Being aware of our "unhealthy norms" enables us to see any red flags waving that remind us of a past *failed* relationship.

Being creatures of habit, we need to:

1- Momentarily focus on past experiences.
2- Become aware of any "unhealthy norms."
3- Have the courage to steer around the approaching rough road of a doomed relationship.

"Think half with your heart,
and half with your head."

My Mom

How do we know if the relationship is doomed? It is easy to determine what lies ahead if you can say, **"I.D.T."** (I Did That.)

If you choose to travel down the same "rough road" over and over and over again, you will fall into the same "potholes" over and over and over again.

How many times over are you going to go down the same road? Don't we usually take a road we're familiar with *because* we know where it leads us? Well, that is great for driving directions, but it is the number one cause for relationships ending up at a dead end.

When we know a street leads to a dead-end, we avoid that route; so, **why don't we have the same navigational abilities with men?** *WE* are supposed to be the ones good at directions (or at least good at asking for directions so that we can successfully get to our destination).

Are you currently traveling down a road that you have traveled before? Did you like where you ended up last time?

Life is full of
C - H - O - I - C - E - S.

If it is your choice to take the same road over and over and over again, then do not complain when you end up at the same place over and over and over again. Duh! **I.D.T.** If you already did *that*, then try something else. It is wiser to try something different in your search of a healthy relationship, than to repeat the same failure many times over. This is nothing more than common sense, no? Who said that when it comes to love we should throw common sense out the window?

Frank and Ernest

Always Something There to Remind Me

Write down the names of all those men that you have dated in the past and see if there are any common threads as to *why* you were attracted to them and *why* the relationships ended.

NAME	WHY ATTRACTED	REASON RELATIONSHIP ENDED

Are you choosing the same looking men?
(Placing no regard on who the man actually is.)

Are you choosing the same personality over and over again?
(Because you are initially attracted to what you're used to.)

Are you comfortable in a relationship because this man reminds you of someone else?
(Perhaps someone you couldn't have.)

Maybe what you are initially attracted to is exactly what the last relationship did not fulfill?
(Choosing to ignore everything else.)

♪

"You're almost afraid to be true to yourself.
Keep your heart open, 'cause love will find a way."

performed by Pablo Cruise

When choosing a mate, you should be aware of any characteristics that fall into your norm. Are the characteristics complementary to who *you* are and what *you* want? Or, have you been down this road before, but believe, "it is going to be different this time." Many women will not acknowledge that they are with someone because he reminds them, on some level, in some way, of someone else.

Be brave. Be okay with yourself and acknowledge the good characteristics you have been attracted to and the bad characteristics that have attracted you for some reason.

Don't make the mistake of choosing a man because of another man in your past. Chapter VIII will help you focus on roles that may be playing havoc with your "significant other" decision.

** Spending time with someone may allow you to fall in love, even though you were not initially attracted to that person. Just as you, spending time with him, will allow him to fall in love with you (quirky imperfections and all).*

If you have sex too soon, your ability to see the relationship for what it truly is may be blurred . After bodily fluids have been shared, there are unknown forces in the universe that impact the relationship. Not giving into the heated moment allows for smarter decisions and, therefore, better consequences. So proceed slowly... sorry, rewind does not exist in relationships. (You can always rely on unshaven legs to thwart your temptation.)

☐ I totally get this chapter.

☐ I should re-read this chapter.

☐ __________ (fill in name) needs to read this chapter.

By being a "chooser" instead of "hoping to be chosen,"
you will increase your chances of getting what you want.

Chapter IV

Check List

IN the battle of the sexes, hands down, women win in the shopping category. So, why don't we use our savvy shopping skills when looking for a man to share our life with?

It seems that ever since Cinderella went into competition with the town's women for the Prince's heart, men are considered the "buyers."

"Buyers" have the choice, yes, but don't the "sellers" have the option of turning down the buyer because the terms of the sale are just not good enough?

If a business consistently sells its goods at an under-valued price, the company will go out of business. What makes women think that if they sign on the dotted line to a less-than-full-value relationship that it, too, will not go bankrupt?

Let's go shopping. If you need a new jacket, you go to the store already knowing what type of jacket you are shopping for, right? Well, women usually spend more time, energy, and thought on the purchase of a new jacket than they do on a new man. Sad, isn't it? Growing up believing in the Cinderella story, we unconsciously think that we are in the running to be *chosen* over other women by "The Man." We fail to recognize that we, too, are buying into something.

We are buying into a life with another individual. What kind of life are you buying into?

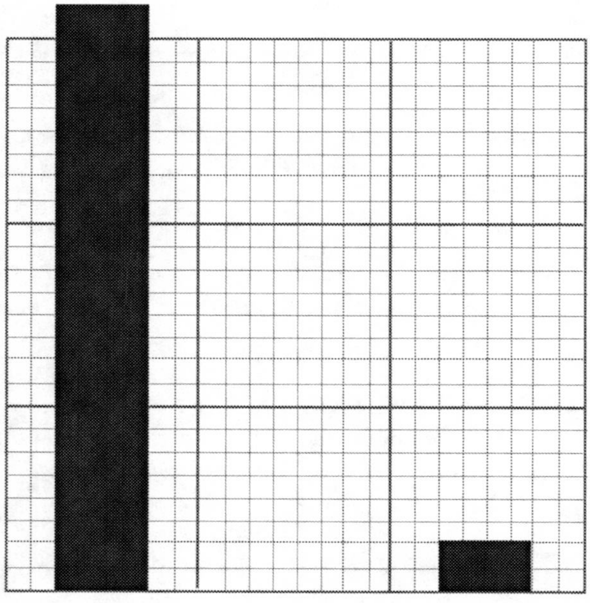
Perceived Statistical Data
source: RAS' Perception
Number of Women who think men will change
Number of Men who actually change

Starting right now, write down all the qualities you are looking for in a man. I do not care if you write down three, seven, or thirty-seven things. The jacket you went shopping for was going to be lightweight, mid-length, a pastel color, belted, and have a collar. Can you name five qualities about the man you are shopping for? Of course we are willing to settle on a slightly different jacket if price dictates, but who wants to shop for a man on the clearance rack? All the picked-over, irregular, or damaged goods are on that rack. And, think about it - a jacket is around for a few years, a marriage is supposed to last a lifetime. Who wants to go through life with a cheap, worn-out, falling apart, irregular fitting, or damaged jacket? No amount of money saved is worth it.

Happily married (not miserably married) is the goal of this shopping trip. Now concentrate on what you are looking for, and remember to revisit the list with every guy that has you saying, "He may be the one."

Please make your own Check List below. After reading all the chapters, you may want to come back and revisit the qualities you are looking for in a mate. I expect you will become more specific as you learn more about yourself.

My Man's Qualities: (What I want now.)	**My Man's Qualities:** (After reading this book.)
______________________	______________________
______________________	______________________
______________________	______________________
______________________	______________________
______________________	______________________
______________________	______________________
______________________	______________________

"Women cannot complain anymore about men until they start showing better taste in them."

Bill Maher

Girls, the old saying goes, "You'd better shop around." There's a truth to that.

Think about this -
When you walk into a shoe department, do you ever pick up a pair of shoes on the nearest display and march right up to the register without first looking around at other choices? Of course not! You definitely look around, find a few different styles you like, try them on in different sizes/colors, and even walk around in them to see how they feel. Then you make a decision on which pair to buy. That's a smart shopper!

So, then, why would you ever, ever, ever march down the aisle to marry the first man that came into your life without knowing how other men treat you, make you feel, or affect your life? Please spend more time shopping for and choosing your husband than you do for your shoes.

☐ I totally get this chapter.
☐ I should re-read this chapter.
☐ __________ (fill in name) needs to read this chapter.

"Happiness is a direction,
not a place."

Chapter V

Don't Look at the Scale; Don't Look at Your Age

HERE is the typical question I get asked from acquaintances: "What is wrong with you?" My reply is always the same: "Excuse me, *wrong* with me?" They cannot understand how I can still be single at 35 years old. These people would prefer that I was a divorced woman to show that at least "I tried."

Tried at what? Failure? Well, I have been living my life, and I am exactly where I am supposed to be. I spent seven years living with a man as if it were a marriage. After our split, who lost out financially? Me. Who had to start over after ripping out the foundation of seven years? Me. I had no business at the age of 22 shacking up with someone going through a divorce and with a child. His problems became my problems. It took the last six years of my life to find out who *I* was, what *I* was worth, and what *I* wanted.

I meet men, date men, have had sex with men (I hope my Dad skips this chapter), break-up with men . . . I have not chosen to marry just because I am a certain "marrying" age in society's mind.

Who is to say at what age after 30, we figure out what we want out of life. (See Chapter IX, *The Quake of 29*.) The "Mister Perfect for Me" does not show up when you are a certain age, or when you lose fifteen pounds, or when you are experiencing a lull in your career, or when you think it is time to start a family.

Every man you spend time with
will teach you something
about yourself.

Notice what you like and what you dislike about each man you meet.

"I married my college boyfriend because
I didn't have enough experience to know that
there could be someone who fit me better.
I was scared to take the chance of losing what I already had.

I wish I had been more courageous and avoided a marriage
that was not a good fit for either of us."

Tara A. Estlin

Notice how you feel about where you are in your life's journey. Be okay with yourself knowing that each day you are making conscious decisions that will promote a healthy environment for you. You can then attract a mate that is doing the same. There you have it - a fabulous mate for a fabulous mate (even if you still have not lost those last fifteen pounds).

☐ I totally get this chapter.

☐ I should re-read this chapter.

☐ ___________ (fill in name) needs to read this chapter.

"When we *think* we are in love,
we avoid listening to advice and common sense."

Chapter VI

The First Two Months Don't Count

BELOW is an email that was sent to me by a hard-working, fun-loving, and pretty 28-year-old woman. **As you read her words, keep in mind that the relationship she is referring to is *only two weeks old*.** Her reaction to the new guy in her life is very common as Dopamine takes its effect.

The pleasure drug that the body produces during courtship that allows us to believe that everything will turn out fine.

> *"He helped me to see that I am beautiful. He has given me security in an uncertain world. I can honestly say he is the most amazing man that has entered my life and I know that I want to be with him and he with me. In my heart I feel that this is right. It is not like all the other ones - not even close."*

Two Months later… the relationship was over.

(Those of us who have felt that same feeling of "never before" multiple times have to smile at our own dopiness.)

The first two months of dating a new guy are very tricky. Whether you are 17 or 37 years of age, this is the part of the relationship that is ALWAYS so confusing.

Why? Because, in addition to Dopamine playing havoc with our brains, most people for the first two months can be *everything* and *anything* to win the affection of the object of their desire -- you!

Evelyn's insecurity spoils the moment.

Making a major decision on a relationship in these first two months is like buying a pair of shoes without trying them on. You are attracted to the shoes, you think they will be a good fit, BUT, what will happen when you actually put them on and walk around in them all day? When the new Mr. Wonderful's real personality starts coming out in that third month - is he a good fit to your personality? . . . or is he like a pair of shoes that hurt your feet?

. . . and why would you want to walk through life with shoes that hurt your feet and make you miserable? We all have bought that beautiful pair of shoes, but after wearing them for longer than an hour, could not wait to take them off. I have even returned them and explained to the salesperson about the blisters, pain, and soreness that they caused. No matter how good they looked, the thought of another experience with them is just not worth the trauma. It amazes me that women do not get rid of lame men just as fast.

Do not judge the quality of this new man in your life during the first two months of dating. What is the title of this chapter? *The First Two Months Don't Count.*

I, too, have dated men that did the expected, thinking to myself, "Wow, this is great!" Of course, two months later, many of these relationships ran their course. The woozy feeling from the attention and the initial mutual attraction was gone. Most men do not understand that they have to court you FOR LIFE. Remember, once "I Do" is said, you are now 50% of each other's happiness or sadness. The flowers, cute little gifts, gentlemanly manners, emotional support, compliments, massages, lovey-dovey messages and e-mails. . . are not supposed to have a 60-day expiration.

Side bar here.

If in these first two months he shows signs of inconsideration, take note of this behavior. Actions will give you incredible insight into what he would verbally tell you *if he could.* When he does not call for a week because he is busy with work, family, friends, *(whatever the excuse),* he is telling you something. He is telling you that he is not interested in having you as a big part of his life *right now.* He may like you, but his priorities are elsewhere. What I want you to focus on is the following: if you proceed to think about this man, go out of your way for this man, obsess about this man, and not keep your options open, you are setting yourself up for failure. He has *in his own way* said that a relationship with you is not important to him at this time in his life. Will it ever be? I doubt it. **Boyfriends who are inconsiderate do not grow into considerate husbands.** Let us remember that his signature on the marriage certificate does not mean he decided to change into an attentive, caring, adoring, loving, sharing, and considerate individual. Be sure he has those qualities BEFORE you marry him.

Watch how the dynamics of the relationship change at this two to three month point. Be aware of the changes in yourself and in the man you are dating. Are there more and more things you absolutely adore about him? . . . or more and more things that are absolutely never going to be complementary to you? If he thinks he "has you," and the courting stops, and his considerate behavior towards you fades out. . . ***oops,*** comfortableness has set in. THIS is what you need to see. What is his norm? Do you like this norm? Do not worry about what HE is thinking. He did not think to ask you if it was alright to stop the courtship and just settle for what he truly is - so you decide if this works for YOU. If not, buh-bye. Next! Move on girl. Do not waste a year looking away from his negative behaviors. Why is it that women have a hard time acknowledging what is right smack in front of their faces?

Because, we think we are different than the other girls he has dated. And, we're right. We are different. The problem, however, is he is not different, and never will be, with or without us. Stop making every relationship in your life like pulling teeth. **If a man wants to be with you, he'll make sure he sees you. If he wants to see you smile, he will do what it takes to lift your spirits. It is just that simple.**

DO NOT make excuses for his behaviors. If he does not make your birthday special, it was not a priority to him. It is just that simple. If you decide to marry him and down the road have children with him, do not expect him to make Mother's Day special either. You were well aware of his typical actions BEFORE you married him. You will come to resent him for not being the man you thought you fell in love with...

Oops! There is a MAJOR problem with this train of thought. YOU chose this kind of man, *even* after you saw his true qualities exposed - or should I say - lack of quality exposed. Do you really want to go through life being reminded every day that you chose poorly when it came to a mate? This is not a one-night prom date that you will laugh about in years to come.

♪

"Bouncin' 'round from cloud to cloud,
I got the feelin' like I'm never gonna come down."

performed by Santana with Alex Band

Be honest with him and yourself about what you like and what you do not like. Nobody passes the mind reading test. Tell him what is important to you, and see if he uses that insight to ***continually*** make your world a better, happier, and prettier place.

****For his ever-enduring and loving courtship****

You should want to let your husband know (for the rest of his life) that he is the "most incredible man in the world." (See Chapter XIII, *Reciprocity*.)

So girlfriends, do not put up a front in the beginning of a relationship. No false advertising. If you are loud and gregarious, do not act demure and think, "this is what will attract him." If he says something you disagree with, speak up. Just as you want to see what he is really made of, let him see what you are really made of - just avoid exposing every single one of your flaws on the first date. (Major turnoff.) Give him a chance to learn all about what makes you so special.

A difference in the typical perspectives~

Girl Meets Boy: *We're head over heels "in love" with some guy from afar. He's "perfect" (so we think). We go out with Mr. Make-Me-Weak-in-the-Knees and begin to notice characteristics we do not really care for. This could be anything from the way he chews his food to his habit of getting drunk and starting fights.*

So he just dropped a few notches on the "He's Perfect Scale." How many more notches will he drop in the First Two Months? This is for you to determine.

YOU have the power to pace the relationship.

Boy Meets Girl: *He is interested because you are a girl, and he is attracted to you for some reason: you're pretty, you're smart, you're easily controlled to feed his ego, or maybe he's horny, lonely, and needs company. Whatever the reason may be, whether it is genuine or not, on his rating scale, you do not start at the top. It is ONLY when you have spent time with this man that you garner worth in his eyes. Sleeping with him on the first date usually does not bring you up a notch!*

If you want a man to view you as something of value, understand that ***YOU have the power to pace*** *the relationship in order to give him the time needed to "elevate" his perspective of you.*

☐ I totally get this chapter.

☐ I should re-read this chapter.

☐ __________ (fill in name) needs to read this chapter.

"It takes two to speak the truth - one to speak and another to hear."

Henry David Thoreau

Chapter VII

Listen, Listen, Listen

WOMEN do not listen. We do not listen to our intuition or to the words that come out of a man's mouth. If we did, we would hear during the first date with this new guy the very nuance about him that we will not be able to tolerate in the future.

Stupid me. I sat on a first date thinking the man across the table from me had no social manners -- a quality in a mate which is very important to me. What made me think he had no table manners? After eating half of a cantaloupe, he picked up the skin and slurped up the juice loudly. Of course, I continued to see him. Duh. Each time he slurped his coffee, sucked his fingers at the table, belched loudly, or took enormous mouthfuls of food, I reminded myself that I saw this trait on the first date. I chose poorly when I decided to keep seeing him on and off for a year. Remember, it is not what you love about him that will cause the break-up. (See Chapter XVI, *Who Cares What You Love About Him.*)

Stupid me. I met a man (in this case a Wimp - see Chapter XX) who told me that he loved independent women. He also told me that he was going through a selfish stage, for he was separated from a wife who had controlled his life. I decided to date him. Duh. You do not date a man unless he is single -- I mean divorce papers in hand.

Oh, and when he said he was going through a selfish stage - where were my ears? When a man says he loves independent women, run as fast as you can. What I have come to understand is that if a man believes you are independent, it releases him from any "responsibility." He does not have to feel responsible for you, support you emotionally or financially, or care for your well-being. You are "independent" - why would you need *anything*? Basically, these men want a woman to meet their needs *when it is convenient*. They are not looking for a true union or nurturing companionship. Again, I chose poorly. Everyone in my life told me he was bad news. I was too close to see it.

♪

"I'm the voice you never listen to,
And, I had to break your heart to make you see,
That he's the one who will be missing you,
And, you'll only miss the man
That you wanted him to be."

performed by Chely Wright

I knew he made me feel awful, but I continued to make excuses for him in addition to the ones he made for himself. Even his co-workers had told me what a selfish individual he was. . . my brain must have been on vacation.

Smart me. I went on a date with a guy that seemed consumed with making money. I made a mental note to be aware of this on the next date. Sure enough, on the next date, I listened to his words as he confirmed and reconfirmed how work and money consumed his time. I also learned that he had no long-term relationship experience. (He was 32 years old, and his longest relationship was less than a year.) Of course, he had the work excuses for no serious relationships. How smart was I? Extremely smart. I know that I cannot be with a man that is all work and no play. I also know that relationships take practice, which he has had none of at this time in his life. The conclusion? He is not for me.

Will I go on another date with him? No. If he wants to join a group of friends out for dinner, that's fine. He is not a bad person. He is just not the lid to fit my pot (Chapter XI). I now know not to waste time going down this road. It would have been a poor decision on my part, and I would have been setting myself up for failure.

I have learned to listen to myself and to the men I date. *Have you?*

If that lil' inner voice is screaming, "Wrong!" then it would be in your best interest to listen, listen, listen. If you are in a new relationship and something is just not right, have the courage to walk away and have faith in your journey. How can you expect a relationship to be successful if it does not have a strong foundation? If you are one of the lucky few in the small percentage that defies the odds, good for you. But, most of us will not.

♪

"Many is the guy who told me he cares,
But, they were scratchin' my back, cause I was scratchin' theirs."

from "My Own Best Friend"
performed in Chicago the Musical

A bad start to a relationship is a set up for failure. If you are sneaking around with your new man because he's married or because your family and friends won't approve, what makes you think this is a good thing? Why aren't you in a relationship where you can dance down the street screaming, "I've got one fabulous guy!" When you are in a healthy relationship, you can love out loud. Loving out loud means that you are proud of your relationship choices and have no need to hide who is in your life and what you are doing with that individual.

☐ I totally get this chapter.

☐ I should re-read this chapter.

☐ __________ (fill in name) needs to read this chapter.

Today, I am playing the role of ______________

Tomorrow, I will be content playing the role of ________________

Next year, I hope to play the role of _______________

30 years from now, I will be playing the the role of _____________

Chapter VIII

What Role Are You Auditioning for?

What role <u>are</u> you auditioning for?

His Mom
His Caretaker
His Maid
His Cook
His Mistress
His Assistant
His Shadow
His Daughter
His Sister
His Fling for Now
His Sex Partner
His Punching Bag
His Default Girlfriend
His Teacher
His Student
His Nurse
His Traveling Partner

Or . . . His Lover, Best Friend, and Life-Long Companion?

Make a decision. What you wish for and what you are willing to settle for, will come to fruition.

Do you need him, want him, or love him?

Everyone surrounding the two of you will know the answer to this question before you do.

What role do you want the man in your life to play?

Think of it this way - when you're driving too closely behind a big truck, it is impossible to see what lies ahead of you down the road. Now, if you were to slow down and pull back from the truck, your vision of the road would improve. So, your friends and family, who are along side of you, will see the relationship road you're heading down while you're caught up in the euphoria of having a boyfriend.

What need does he satisfy for you? What need do you satisfy for him? Are these healthy needs? Ha! There is no such thing. If you NEED his financial assistance--***strike one***. If you NEED him in order to feel attractive--***strike two***. If you NEED him to further your career--***strike three, YOU'RE OUT!!*** Oh, but there is more. If you NEED him to not be lonely--***strike four***. If you NEED to feel needed--***strike five***. If you NEED (or shall we say use) him for good sex--***strike six***. *Are we getting the picture here?*

Needing him because he fulfills one or more of your current sappy needs (or because you fulfill one or more of his current sappy needs) is setting yourself up for failure. Your needs will change. When your "new need" is not being met by the man who only fulfilled your "old need," you may feel trapped or resentful.

Feeling trapped or resentful are two very common complaints in unhappy marriages. Feeling trapped will lower your self-esteem. When you believe that you have no control over your own life, how can you feel good about who you are? Then, resentment towards your man grows and eventually squashes sexual attraction. Resentment has a way of unconsciously creeping into a person's psyche. When we resent the man in our life for anything (i.e., verbal abuse, disregard, lack of ambition, negativity, or forgetting to do all the things that remind us how beautiful we are), sex becomes an exercise of "going through the motions," even if at one time you could not sleep at night because you ached to be intimate with this man.

Did you ever notice that the bride and groom figurines
that stand on the top of the wedding cake are
next to each other rather than one in front of the other?

Be very careful about which role you choose. As time goes by, your preferences may change. Perhaps this man will become unable to fill the necessary slot in your life because, do not forget, he has also chosen a slot for you! *Ooohhh* . . . something to think about.

Marry the man that is healthy for you to love with all of your heart, mind, and soul.

Listen to your innermost being. It will tell you whether the two of you are in harmony. Listen to the sixth sense that we women are blessed with, even if it tells you what you don't want to hear . . . that there is something just not right with your relationship. Courage is needed here, girlfriend, if you desire a love that will sustain a marriage.

☐ I totally get this chapter.

☐ I should re-read this chapter.

☐ __________ (fill in name) needs to read this chapter.

"Oh, I'm too young to get married.
Seriously. I'm 22 years old.
It's so annoying that they put pressure on you."

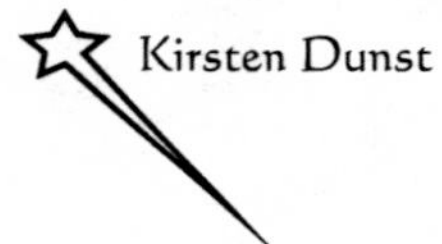

Kirsten Dunst

Chapter IX

The Quake of Twenty-Nine

I cannot stress the importance of this chapter enough. "The Quake of Twenty-Nine" could have been the title of this book.

In our early twenties, we *all think* we know what we want and have great faith in our ability to plan out our lives. You have heard it before, "I want to be married by 25 and have two children by 30." At 23, many of us long to play house. Oh, the joy of setting up house with our boyfriend!

What if I were to tell you that between 27 and 29 years old, "everything you want in life" goes through serious scrutiny? What if I were to tell you that if you were to make a major life decision prior to age 30, like choosing your life-long companion, there is a BIG chance you (or he) may change your mind?

Why take the risk? (Unless you believe that the vow of marriage should not include the phrase "until death do us part.")

This cycle in today's world is out of control. How is it that people can have children with two or three different spouses (or those they are just living with) and yet have so little regard for the negative impact it has on a child? "The kids adjust so well." Yeah right. (OK, we're not going to get into divorced and blended families here. There are plenty of books on that subject as well.)

Nobody warned me about the Quake of 29, so, I set up house when I was 22 with my boyfriend who was 30. Of course, he had great biceps and a motorcycle and I loved him. Sounds mature, doesn't it? Six years later, at the age of 28, those great biceps were not what I focused on anymore.

"We hoped to create this extraordinary bond together.
The problem is we were just too young,
and we weren't right for each other."

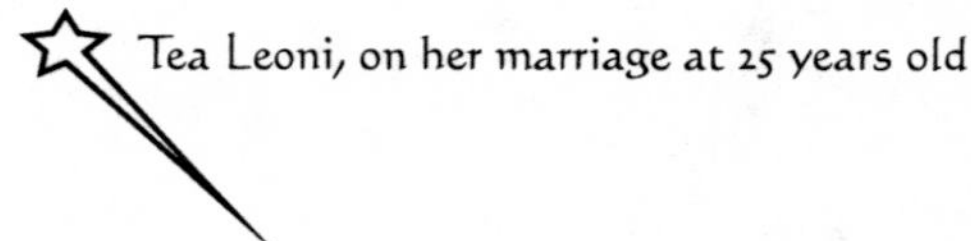
Tea Leoni, on her marriage at 25 years old

"We realized how well we worked together.
We encouraged each other's strengths
and supported each other's weaknesses."

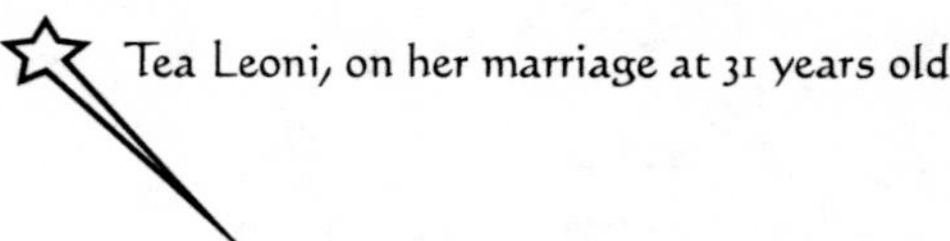
Tea Leoni, on her marriage at 31 years old

Did I love him? Absolutely. He was a good man. Did I resent him? Yes! Imagine that! I had matured over the time we were together, and I began to think about where I was in my life and where I wanted to be in ten years. Was I on the right path?

(Gasp!) The ground shook! The foundation I once stood on cracked open! He was comfortable with his lifestyle; I was not. I did not want to live in his world, and he was uncomfortable in mine. Remember, no relationship is worth more than having a sense of self.

Life continues on past the "I just want to have a boyfriend" stage! This was definitely an aftershock!

You will know when the Quake of 29 hits. Somewhere between age 27 and 29, the firm ground on which you once stood (envisioning your future) will begin to shake. We all, both male and female, go through a metamorphosis. We look at what we have not yet accomplished, and ask ourselves, "What do I want to be when I grow up?" with more urgency. You will look at:

1) Who you are at the moment,
2) Where you are in your life, and most importantly,
3) Whether the choices you have made are fulfilling (and fulfilling enough to stay on this path).

It is strange how our likes and dislikes change during this metamorphosis. What we absolutely "loved" at 23 will be cast aside for what represents us now, what we have become, or what we wish to grow into.

metamorphosis n. - change

♪

"Your love is lifting me higher . . ."

performed by Rita Coolidge

Maybe you went to law school for your parents and they wanted you to marry a lawyer. At approximately 29 years old, you may not be so fulfilled with that legal career or your lawyer husband. You have just realized that you would be happier living in a small town teaching art to third graders. You will not be a good mate for anybody if you are not content with yourself. And, you will start resenting your spouse for everything you're not, but desire to be. You may be in a BIG hurry for the wedding, husband, kids . . . *but, guess what?*

Love does not conquer all. Sometimes it's just like bubblegum on the bottom of our shoes, holding us to a place in our life that is not in our best interest. You have the rest of your life to be married. That is a long time to deal with another person's idiosyncrasies. It is also a long time to listen to the man sleeping next to you snoring in your ear night after night.

Time spent on our own is where we tend to work on our own growth. Maybe it is because we are not wrapped up in someone else's life and actually have the time to focus on our own goals. Reread Chapter Two. Use your twenties to determine your self-worth. Set yourself up for success in life and success in love.

If you haven't made a commitment to yourself, what makes you think you're prepared to make a commitment to someone else?

Give yourself the best marriage gift possible. Time.

> **Time for you to discover**
> **who you are,**
> **who you want to become,**
> **how you want to live,**
> **and if your selected partner has complementary desires.**

Which will you choose?

Choose your future husband as a woman, not as a girl. Making a decision at 23 regarding the man with whom you want to spend the rest of your life is like making that decision as a high school freshman. Yes, you're slightly older and slightly wiser, but the self-development IS JUST NOT THERE. (Sorry, don't blame me; I didn't lay out the course of personal growth.) Why marry "Mr. OK for right now," when at 29 you will probably say, "I'm sorry honey, but I didn't know what I really wanted at 23 years old. I'm a different person now, and I guess we just grew in different directions." And, what happens to those women who have never stood on their own two feet? *What if they went from Mommy & Daddy to Husband?* Those women usually do not have the courage to leave a bad situation. Their hearts are no longer happy and they feel "stuck."

A happy heart promotes a healthy body.

Carrying around a "heavy heart" for a long period of time is not healthy. If the man you choose has a bad attitude and dumps negativity into your world, don't you think there is going to be an effect on your stress level? Don't you think there is going to be an effect on your immune system? You cannot go back and start over. Why walk out on the gangplank *(as if you are blindfolded)*, where you will need to be rescued before drowning in the waves of an unhappy relationship? Let's not rush to say "I Do" only to find ourselves in our early thirties as one more divorce statistic. Let's choose wisely from the beginning.

Everybody wants to believe that they will be the one to defy the odds. If that were true, Las Vegas would not be cashing in on the millions of dollars that it does each weekend. Will there be a small percentage of winners? Yes. Will there be a small percentage of couples that marry in their twenties and live happily together until death do us part? Yes. It is your choice as to whether you want to risk the only hand you have to play, or should I say, give away. Good luck.

☐ I totally get this chapter.
☐ I should re-read this chapter.
☐ __________ (fill in name) needs to read this chapter.

Impatience leads to foolishness.

Chapter X

No More "What Ifs"

THERE are actually issues that are much more serious than the Valentine's Day freak out that occurs in some women's minds. It is as if their entire worth is determined by whether or not they have a guy to take them to dinner on the day that roses cost $17 a piece. Or, what about those women who get depressed because they have no one to kiss at midnight on New Year's Eve! No, it is not the end of the world, but these same women have a tendency to be motivated by fears.

Will you choose marriage based on one of the following fears?

Fear #1
You will never find a man who truly loves you.
(So you will settle for the less-than fabulous boyfriend you currently have.)

Fear #2
You will be alone.
(So you will grab onto any man who will marry you.)

Fear #3
You will never make it financially.
(Therefore you feel forced to marry as soon as possible.)

Fear #4
You will never find someone "in time" to start a family.
(So you will have a child with a man whom you know will not make a good father.)

And finally, the new fear.
Fear #5
That tomorrow will not come.

Do you want just any warm body
next to you at night?

The new fear has been brought on by the 9/11/01 terrorist attacks on America, on-going war, and natural disasters around the globe. How many fearful women, both young and old, have run into the nearest masculine arms and pledged their love? In the face of overwhelming tragedy, it is human nature to want a connection with another person. The man who wraps his arms around you and allows you to feel "safe" *for the moment* may not be the man for you to marry.

Tomorrow will always come.

Are you living for all that life offers or are you making life choices in fear of death? Are you making choices because of "what if...?"

What you have to ask yourself is, "If he wasn't 'good enough' to marry on September 10, 2001 - what makes him the right one to marry now?" If you are rushing to say "I Do" out of fear, in two years, will you find yourself sleeping next to a man you knew was only a Mister-Right-Now kind of guy? (The kind of guy that merely had the capability of filling the *Saturday Night Date* slot.)

☐ I totally get this chapter.
☐ I should re-read this chapter.
☐ __________ (fill in name) needs to read this chapter.

♪

"Find a man who loves you inside and out."

performed by the Bee Gees

Chapter XI

The BIG FOUR

MAGIC. It feels magical when you meet a guy whose very presence puts a beautiful, dreamy haze over your world. You smile more, laugh more, and take on the radiant glow that is inherently produced by feelings of "love."

Ahhhh. . . when you're in the dreamy world of romantic sunsets, lazy mornings in bed, and sipping piña coladas on a Hawaiian honeymoon, the magical euphoria of love is all you need to succeed with your mate.

Sorry to break up the party, ladies.
Let's cut to real life.

Will opposites attract? Yes. Will opposites eventually repel? Yes. Yes. Yes. Opposite anything can be the force that breaks down a relationship over time. You need to decide. Is he Mr. Today or Mr. Forever? Are you in a relationship for the short term or do you want to have a relationship built on a strong foundation, one that will support the life you will be constructing with your man? No two people will agree on everything, but finding your complementary mate is accomplished by partnering with a man who looks at life similarly to the way you do. It is your decision, and your decision alone, as to how much you are willing to bend in order to be with your guy. Choose wisely. You will be bending for a lifetime. Ask yourself, "Can I tolerate this for the next 20, 40, or 60 years?"

Remember, it's not only what you love about him that will determine whether you are happy or miserable in your marriage. (See Chapter XVI, *Who Cares What You Love About Him*.)

vow *v.*
to make a solemn (a very serious) promise

This is it girls! If you ignore one of the following Big Four Factors, you are setting yourself up for divorce court, where misery, sadness, and discontentment will be your companions. You will have a beautiful marriage ceremony only to later face the awful dilemma of:

> *(In a desperate, crying voice)*
> *"Do I have to deal with this man for the rest of my life?*
>
> *Even though he refuses to go to the family events that I cherish?*
>
> *Even though he wants to sit on the couch in his free time when I want to participate in outdoor activities?*
>
> *Even though he won't go to church with me?*
>
> *Even though he continues to drink when he promised me he'd quit???"*
>
> ____
>
> ____
>
> (Fill in your own above. These are some common complaints I have heard.)

Aauugghh!!!! This will leave you feeling powerless, powerless, powerless. (And, you had better pray that there are no children involved when you get to this place!)

NEW THOUGHT PROCESS

Do yourself a favor and say this out loud frequently: "I am smart, courageous, and I deserve to find the lid that fits my pot."
(This shall become your personal oath.)

Some women have said,
"What if I only have 1, 2, or 3 factors
in common with my boyfriend?"

You tell me -
does it sound like a set-up for a successful relationship?

"Finding the lid that fits your pot" means marrying the complementary mate that will promote a healthy environment in which you both will thrive. Everybody talks about "finding their match," but obviously, the greater percentage of the population is clueless on what that truly means. It is vital to your well being to link up with a complementary mate.

Here's a visual for you. For a moment, think of wrenches. Yes, I mean a whole set of all different-sized wrenches.

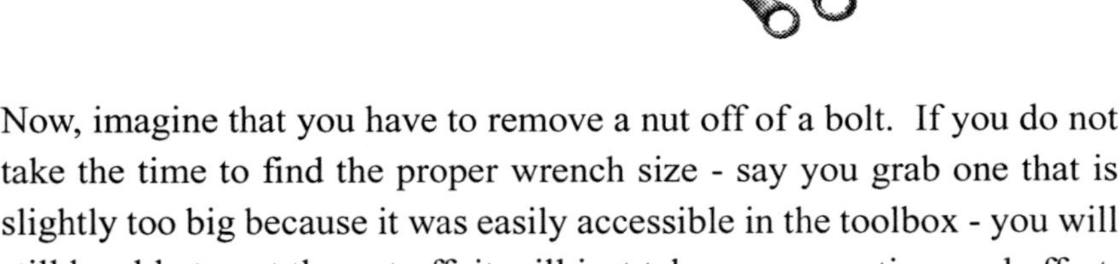

Now, imagine that you have to remove a nut off of a bolt. If you do not take the time to find the proper wrench size - say you grab one that is slightly too big because it was easily accessible in the toolbox - you will still be able to get the nut off, it will just take you more time and effort.

If you had taken the time to go through the toolbox to find the proper sized wrench, the nut would have come off the bolt much more easily. Less frustration. Satisfaction achieved.

By the way, men are not the nuts here. In fact, it is women who are nuts for not choosing their companions wisely!

END OF THE DRAMA

Scene 17. SOMETIME AFTER THE FIRST SIXTY DAYS

BOTTLE OF CHAMPAGNE
(after pausing to reflect on her needs)
Sorry, but this isn't a reality show where after only weeks I claim that you're the man for me. It was great hanging out with you for awhile, but I'm not interested in taking this relationship any further. After meeting and dating many different men, I have come to realize that it is BRUT men that complement me.

CAN OF BEER
(Shaking his head slightly up & down)
I was hoping it could work out for us - I really like you. But, you're right, we are different in so many ways and that has caused too many silly arguments. My mother always said that six-pack girls are more my style!

BOTTLE OF CHAMPAGNE
(getting choked up)
Best of luck to you. See you around.

CAN OF BEER
Best of luck to you too.

The two embrace in a good-bye hug.
FADE OUT

You have the power to say "Yes" or "No." Remember, this man will be 50% of your happiness or sadness. Your goal should be a loving commitment to a partnership that has the potential to go the *distance*.

Here we go. The Big Four Factors. I encourage you to take notes in the margins.

Are you a couch potato or a social butterfly?
It does not take a rocket scientist to figure out that couch potatoes go better with couch potatoes. If you are a social butterfly and you marry a couch potato, how much time will you two spend arguing, resenting one another, or at opposite ends of town? Human beings are creatures of habit and the clash of your habits will get in the way of a harmonious relationship.

Dragging him to a party where he sits in a corner
IS NOT going to make you happy.
Staying at home night after night
IS NOT going to make you happy.
Arguing with him that he is not social enough
IS NOT going to make you happy.

See? You will get mad at him for making you unhappy, BUT you, Ms. Butterfly, chose to marry him, **AND you knew** that he was a couch-loving, stay-at-home mole. Maybe moles are gregarious, but only in their own holes. On the flip side, Ms. Happy-at-Home Mole, do yourself a favor and do not marry the 24/7 party guy.

Compatibility Factor Number 1:
Do "we" match-up Socially?

- ☐ Yes.
- ☐ Nope.
- ☐ Not sure.
  I need to discuss this with him.

Your comfort level in the social structure is also very important. Now, I am not talking about high teas and yacht parties versus hanging out in the local bar every night. I am talking about how you prefer to live your life and how that affects your friendships and relationships. Is it more often your choice to have dinner out at a nice restaurant or to simply grab a burger and fries at a drive-thru? What would your man choose more often? Do your lifestyle preferences match up? . . . or, will you choose to disregard the difference now and eventually get fed-up with Mr. Super Size Me?

Others can often see what is right smack in front of our faces while we are too busy looking the other way or looking in the mirror to make sure we look good for the wrong guy. Over time, this social factor can make or break a marriage. I believe in stacking the deck for the best odds. **Choose the man that complements you socially.**

Dopamine, norepinepherine and phenylethylmine. *What???*

The chemistry between two people boils down to these hard-to-spell and hard-to-pronounce words. Yeah, and you thought it was that inexplicable magic that happens when two people are attracted to each other. Oh, the rapid heartbeat and the euphoria of being in love. Like I said, it all comes down to the brain's three love chemicals. That is why when we have chemistry with a new guy, we stay up late and talk to him for hours on the phone, lose our appetites, and have increased energy. (The next time you complain that you need to lose weight, don't go on a diet--just fall in "chemistry" with someone.)

OK, so you have chemistry with your mate. **Girls, do not confuse sexual attraction for an emotional connection.**

Question:

Do you know why a wedding ring is always worn
on the finger, next to your pinky, of the left hand?

Answer:

It was once thought to be the site of the vein of love.
The vein: a lifeline.
(Who are you choosing to be your "loveline?")

Sex alone does not provide the closeness that a healthy emotional environment supports. I do not care how good the sex is. Emotional intimacy is just as important as sexual attraction. You need both for your relationship to go the distance! Matching only from the hips down will give your relationship about two years of oxygen, and a meeting only of the minds will leave you physically love-starved. Who wants to be in a marriage where you will find yourself desiring more than what you settled for? *Hmm . . . Not me!*

Let's actually talk about some issues surrounding sex.

I am not going to preach here whether or not you should abstain from sex before marriage. That is each person's independent decision. I do believe in waiting to have sex until the age of 21 though, when wiser partnering, pregnancy protection, and STD prevention decisions can be made. You will be having sex for the rest of your life; there is no need to hop in bed and make a bad decision THAT CANNOT BE UNDONE. Unfortunately, there is no rewind button on any of you that can be pressed to undo what you did last night, last week, or last month.

But, how important is sex in a marriage? I am sure that if you ask many people the answers will widely vary. I believe that sex is one of the BIG Four Factors that will make or break your relationship. Why is it that people want to believe that if one partner likes to have sex five times a week and the other partner likes to have sex once a week, all is going to be OK in paradise? One or both of the partners are going to be continually unhappy. How long can unhappiness go on in one area before it spills into other areas of the relationship?

You are kidding yourself and your future mate if sex is not considered when analyzing your relationship foundation. There is a lid for every pot. So, find the lid that sexually fits your pot.

Compatibility Factor Number 2:
Do "we" match-up Sexually?

- ☐ Yes.
- ☐ Nope.
- ☐ Not sure.
I need to discuss this with him.

Keep it simple. If you are not a sexual person, then choose a mate that does not consider sex a high priority. If you are dating someone who is highly sexual, do not pretend that you are, just to make the other person happy. You cannot pretend forever. If sexual compatibility is a high priority for you, be sure to test-drive that car before you buy it. *(Wink wink.)* If you have chosen to wait until marriage, please discuss your attitude towards sex with your future mate.

Do you like the way he kisses? Do you like the way he smells? *Don't laugh! Your relationship stands little chance if you do not connect on this level.* The way a man smells will turn you on or turn you off! Do you like the way he touches you? There are plenty of good books out there about how to be a good lover. Read them! Buy a few for him too.

It is important to choose the man that is on the same page as you when it comes to sexual likes and dislikes.

compatibility

$ Financially $

I am sure you have heard it said that most couples fight about money. I am sure you have also heard it said that you should marry for love and *not* money. What is important when choosing a mate is that you AGREE on money -- how it should be earned, spent, and how it should be saved. What type of living status do you desire? What type of living status does he desire?

Everybody has his or her own priorities when it comes to holding on to and letting go of money. If you and your mate disagree on this factor, you are setting the stage for resentment.

If your future frugal husband is content to live in a one-bedroom apartment for the rest of his life and you decide to marry him knowing that this will NEVER do for you, you are choosing poorly.

Compatibility Factor Number 3:
Do "we" match-up Financially?

- ☐ Yes.
- ☐ Nope.
- ☐ Not sure.
  I need to discuss this with him.

He may be a nice guy who would never cheat on you, but YOUR dream is to live in a three-bedroom house, even if it means having a smaller savings account. Did you forget to discuss those details with him? Or did you find out his goals and then pretend in your head that you would change his mind later? (See Chapter XIV, *Down the Road.*)

Pay attention to how each of you spends money. If he thinks your spending habits are ridiculous now, when you get married you will be sneaking shopping bags through the back door so that he does not see them and start a fight. Why would you say "I Do" to someone who does not agree with your views on spending, saving, and investing money? I dated a guy who had no problem spending $80 on a bottle of wine, but was too cheap to buy me a $14 beach chair. An acquaintance's husband would not blink at purchasing a $150,000 Tiffany lamp, but refused to take her out to fancy restaurants. He said they were a waste of money. We each view spending money differently. Figure it out girls! Figure out if the two of you agree on money spent on cars, money saved for vacations, money needed for healthcare, money spent on a pet's vet bills, and the incredible amont of money spent on beauty supplies.

Beware: These "everyday things" that are rarely addressed during courtship can pick away at a marriage over time.

Talk about money BEFORE you walk down the aisle. As soon as you become serious with a man, talk about each of your debts and assets. People can comfortably talk about everything under the sun, including sex, but when it comes to discussing the details of a person's salary, bank account, or credit history, it is considered intrusive. Do not be afraid to speak up! Remember, money matters big time in marriage and your habits need to be in alignment with your mate's.
Choose a man that complements you financially.

Why would you choose a man
who does not
see the world as you do?

compatibility

It amazes me when couples think that spirituality is not important in a marriage. I often hear comments like, "We are not religious so it doesn't matter." This is such surface thinking. I am not going to analyze different religious beliefs, but I do want to address the fact that spirituality affects our daily decisions, our values, our outlook on life, even our thoughtfulness vs. selfishness, our hopes, our dreams, and our ability to face each day when the world does not feel like a happy place.

Faith. To have a happy partnership, you must look at how you and your partner deal with that word. What do you have faith in? Where do YOU place emphasis in your life? God, goodwill, career, family, physical fitness, material possessions, or education?

I want you to be aware of where your life is focused. What does your man put his faith in? Where is the emphasis in his life? When the going gets tough (and it will), are you a negative thinker or a positive thinker? Which one is he?

Again, keep it simple. If you believe in God, marry someone who believes in God. Why would you marry an Atheist? Why would you set the two of you up for the difficulty of a relationship based on two different philosophies? Do you really think that love conquers all? Sorry to tell you, but, uhhh … *Nope!* You may *love* the man that does not match up with you spiritually, but must you marry him? If you plan on having children, how will evolution be explained to them? Relationships are in constant flux. To put one more thing, *especially something as deeply rooted as your faith,* on a collision course with the debate over the organization and order (or lack thereof) of the universe, is hazardous to the health of a relationship.

Compatibility Factor Number 4:
Do "we" match-up Spiritually?

- ☐ Yes.
- ☐ Nope.
- ☐ Not sure.
  I need to discuss this with him.

No matter where you place yourself on the spiritual scale, "old soul," "new soul," or "no soul," being in agreement about the existence of a soul (or not) does matter.
Choose to marry the man that matches you spiritually.

Say this out loud:
"I am smart, courageous,
and I deserve to find the lid that fits my pot."

Keep this promise to yourself. Remain faithful to YOU.

☐ I totally get this chapter.
☐ I should re-read this chapter.
☐ __________ (fill in name) needs to read this chapter.

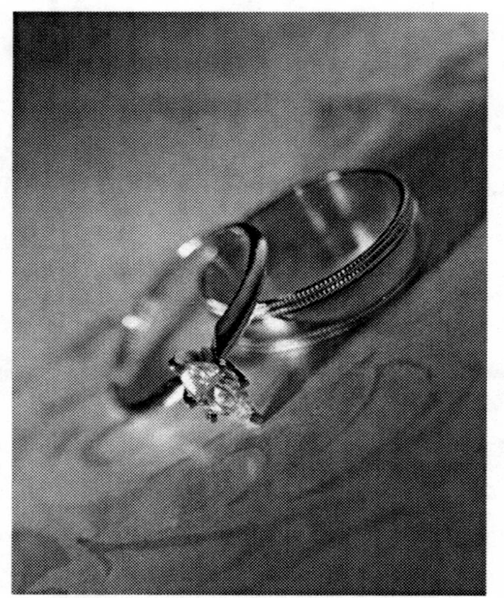

Chapter XII

Stop Doing Cartwheels, Back Flips, and Somersaults

CARTWHEELS, back flips, and somersaults. Oh, this was me, big time. You would have thought I was really good at gymnastics, twisting myself into whatever I thought "he" would like and find attractive ("he" being whomever I had my eye on at the moment). I became interested in motorcycles, country music, basketball, baseball, golf . . . whatever the "he" in my life was into. Just think of me as the sappiest of the sappiest; I would dress the part, learn about the sport or hobby, spend more than a healthy amount of time with him and his interests, and gee, somehow forget to put effort and time into MY interests.

A girl can only perform this gymnastic routine for so long.

**Having a relationship
is NOT more important than having a self.**

As a couple, your lives intersect through interaction. The important question to ask is, "Do we have an optimal mix of togetherness and individuality?" Only a balance of "We" time and "I" time will lead to a fulfilling union.

At many wedding ceremonies, they speak about the symbolism of the rings: the unending circle. I believe a circle represents each person in a relationship. When we become involved with a man, our circle will overlap his circle in one of four ways. This is what I call "The Circle Theory." Let's look to see if you and your man have a healthy balance of "We" and "I" in your relationship.

Find yourself in one of the following four descriptions . . .

Successful relationships require a unique arithmetic:

1 Whole Person
+ 1 Whole Person
= 1 Successful Relationship

This is different than the "you complete me" philosophy of:

½ person
+ ½ person
= 2 jealous, resentful, unfulfilled individuals with low self-esteem

(Notice that they are complete circles.)

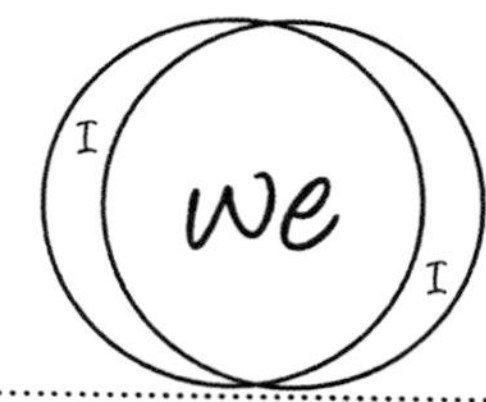

The "We" Couple

If you are inseparable from the first day you meet, no longer have time for your friends, are predominantly only interested in what HE is interested in, are saying, "I love you" after two weeks, and are planning to set up house with each other after three months--THIS IS YOU.

LOOK AT THE CIRCLES! It is easy to see that there is not enough "I" for either person in this union. Denying yourself something that you enjoy and then resenting him for your "sacrifices" is not the path to take for happily-ever-after. This tends to be the I/We connection that most twenty-somethings fall into. (Yep, I did it too.) And, we all know at least one girl who no longer has time to hang with her friends because she has become one with her latest boyfriend.

Just because you love each other and enjoy being a couple, does not mean either of you should be denied the things you enjoy in life.

Are you in a relationship that is causing your *self* to become nonexistent?

If you are in a relationship where there is too much "We" and not enough "I" time, be brave enough to put on the brakes. A stronger "I" actually allows for a more gratifying "We." Examine your own situation and discover what you think, feel, and want to do with your life. **Be sure that whatever is important to YOU is a part of your life when you are with your man.**

** Phone calls, text messaging, and instant messaging do not qualify as "We" time. When you are looking forward to a hug and a kiss from your man, "XOX" or "ILU" or "IMU" showing up in your Inbox just isn't the same as the real thing.*

The 'I'm for Me and You're for Me Too' Couple

Are you conforming to *his* wants and *his* needs? I have three words for you: get a life! Wrapping yourself around a man's life is a gymnastic routine that needs new choreography. *Why is it that your personal desires are not being respected in this relationship?*

I understand that you desire a connectedness and a sense of "belonging" to someone, but if you are repeating patterns of co-dependent behavior, go see a therapist. The title of this book is *what*? *I AM Before "I Do."* Need I say more?

Probably.

What makes you attracted to selfish men, the life-sucking creatures that are the epitome of what we women SHOULD NEVER, EVER, EVER, EVER, ***EVER***, EVER, EVER, EVER, ***EVER***, EVER, MARRY??!! Am I passionate about this particular subject? You better believe it. This self-professed I-Can-Change-Him woman has also been attracted to her fair share of men that possess the ability to suck the life right out of you. I then wondered why I felt so let down.

These men do not make women an integral part of their life. Women are simply a distraction or provide some type of "service." Maybe these men did not have a father figure that respected women. Who knows? *Who cares?* Why spend your energy trying to figure out why a man does not have the ability to be in a healthy relationship? **The bottom line is - do you want a companion who considers your wants and needs, or do you want a man that will always put himself first?** The choice is yours.

"I've learned more about myself in the year since my boyfriend and I split than I did during the two years we were together.

And, I plan to keep learning,
so I don't choose to make the same mistakes
with the next guy that comes into my life."

Patricia Neal

The flip side to a life-sucking man is a life-sucking woman who expects her man to wrap his entire life around her. *Is this you?* Do you expect your man to embrace your life, needs, and wants as more important than his own? If so, stop being so self-centered and give a little. Give your attention to his life. Give the gift of making him feel good about who he is, and realize that it makes him happy to be with you. If you are psychologically draining, you are just as bad as a life-sucking man.

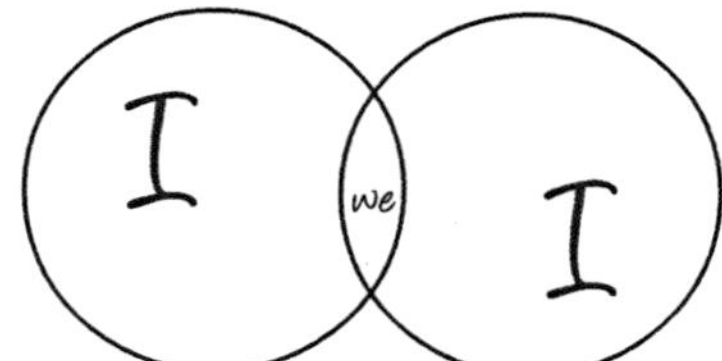

The 'I'm for Me' Couple

Oh my, commitment issues. Big time! Not much teamwork here. It is hard for me to imagine this couple cuddling in bed, on the sofa, or by a fire. There is plenty of "I" time within this relationship. *Too* much "I" time. Without enough "We" time, where is this relationship headed? Nowhere. How long can two people stand in the same place? Definitely not for forever. Time keeps marching on. A stagnant relationship will eventually *feel* like it is going backwards.

If you are in this type of relationship now, ask yourself why. If sex is your answer, then please ask yourself another question: Is that really enough for you? Does this equation make you happy? Will it ten years from now? Remember, only you can answer what role you want your companion, your mate, to play in your life. (See Chapter VIII, *What Role Are You Auditioning for?*)

Do you have the right "mix" in your relationship?

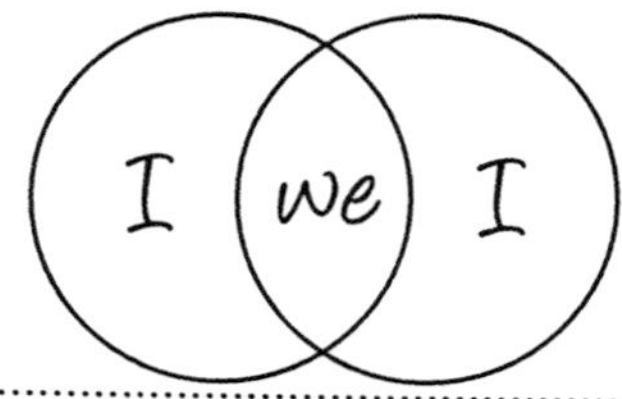

The Healthy Couple

Separate individuals seeking an intimacy with another person.
This is healthy!

This optimal connection is what you want to strive for in your relationship in order to retain happiness in your heart and success in your marriage. You must continue to pursue your personal aspirations, such as education, career advancement, mastering a hobby or sport, or anything else that you have always wanted to do. Nurture your sense of "this is me" while you nurture your relationship.

Your couple time should allow you to share in an activity that you both enjoy and/or a goal that the two of you are striving to reach. For example, I had a boyfriend who suggested that if I learned how to play golf (his hobby), he would learn how to roller-skate (my hobby). It worked. We were able to share in each other's interests. This was a healthy approach to getting what we each wanted. If more women analyzed their I/We situations based upon the Circle Theory, they would wave buh-bye to the not-for-me men. Welcome into your life someone who understands the importance of the following equation:

Personal Time for the Fulfillment of Individual Dreams
+ Couple Time for Collective Goals
= Relationship Bliss

☐ I totally get this chapter.
☐ I should re-read this chapter.
☐ __________ (fill in name) needs to read this chapter.

♪

"No chains,
No strings,
No fences,
No walls,
No net,

Just you to catch me when I fall.
Look heart, no hands."

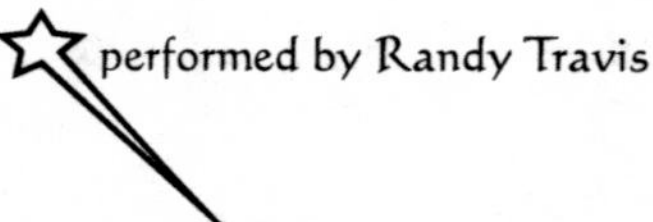
performed by Randy Travis

Chapter XIII

Reciprocity

OPTIMALLY, we decide to get married to share our lives.

A bonding can only take place when we decide to no longer live as a disconnected individual. The vow is a physical, mental, and spiritual commitment. Just like anything else in which one may want to succeed: playing a musical instrument, learning a foreign language, excelling in a sport, or improving eating habits - your mindset is extremely important for a successful marriage. Those that never make the mental commitment to a relationship have planted the seeds for divorce, *even before the "I do's" take place.* Two people need to make this commitment; otherwise, it is like one person rowing the kayak for two . . . eventually the rower's arms get really tired. Why hold on to a man who expects you to do all the rowing? Do not expect him to do all the rowing either.

Reciprocity must be present in even the smallest of daily activities. It is the fuel that re-energizes our spirit, so we can keep outpouring the love that nourishes our relationships.

Reciprocity n. - mutual interchange between two people.

Cute Story

One of my friend's parents shared with me a wonderful example of reciprocity. Five mornings a week, the wife would get her husband coffee as he was getting ready for work. On the two mornings he was not preparing for work, he would bring her coffee in bed. Her simple kind act of making coffee was appreciated by him and reciprocated so that she could also feel loved, cared for, and appreciated.

Do you and your man reciprocate the love and support necessary to continually re-fuel the relationship? A lasting affection, commitment, and partnership are what enable a couple to go the distance. It cannot always be about one person's needs, wants, desires, or dreams. If it is all about him or all about you, someone's heart is going to run out of fuel.

"There is calming beauty
between two people
when loving acts are reciprocated."

Be in tune with how you feel about what your man does for you AND what your man does not do for you. Is he supportive of your goals? Or, is he possessive, controlling, demanding, disrespectful, and negative towards your aspirations? We all need the supportive hand, ear, or nudge in our life. You must ask yourself, "Is the man I am choosing as my companion capable of re-fueling my heart, spirit, and ambition when I need him to?" If he is your best friend, lover, and life-long partner, shouldn't he possess this capability? (The answer is "YES!" for all you women who are now making excuses for the man in your life who does not support the very thing that makes your heart smile.)

Anything that rejuvenates you, or adds some sunshine to your life, should be applauded by your man (and vice versa).

Are we getting this? Reciprocity. Re-fueling. Look for it: from the way he feels about your career, to the way he brings you chocolate when you are PMSing, to the way he treats you in bed . . .

would that be "sexciprocity?" (LOL)

Do you feel loved, loving, or both?

Let me share with you the exact moment I realized that a certain "boyfriend" was incapable of refueling my heart.

> I can remember sitting on his couch and asking him to pump up the basketball in the trunk of my car. As I said the words, I realized that I had never asked him for anything, nor had he been generous with his kindness. I actually felt awkward asking him to do this small favor, because *I knew* it would be a big effort on his part.
>
> As I sat there with my thoughts of loneliness, sadness, and smallness, I thought to myself, "Why am I chosing to be with such a selfish man?"

♪

"Do you love me as I love you?"

performed by Cole Porter

I certainly did not feel love from this man and as the basketball filled with air, my heart deflated.

Younger me did not get rid of Mr. Selfish as quickly as simple common sense would dictate.

I went to his house one night, and he had a bath waiting for me. He even added the touches of fragrant candles and an expensive cabernet. It was the second of three nice things he did for me in a year's time. Three! Thank God I found my brain somewhere between my thoughts of, "I've never wanted to kiss anyone as much as I want to kiss you right now" and "What woman in her right mind would want a man like him for the rest of her life?"

Ewww . . . think about it. If I was married to him and he did his three nice things for me each year - let's give the marriage 40 years - that would add up to 120 nice things during my entire marriage! Oh my. There would be many more days of, "I didn't marry very well" instead of "This man is my sunshine on a cloudy day."

Who do you want to marry - the man that does 120 nice things each year or the man that does 120 nice things in a 40-year period? The choice is yours. My appreciation goes to the men whose loving acts have uplifted my heart and made me smile.

mmm... How sweet life is when your heart is uplifted,
and you cannot help but smile.

☐ I totally get this chapter.
☐ I should re-read this chapter.
☐ __________ (fill in name) needs to read this chapter.

"Be bold in what you stand for and
careful what you fall for."

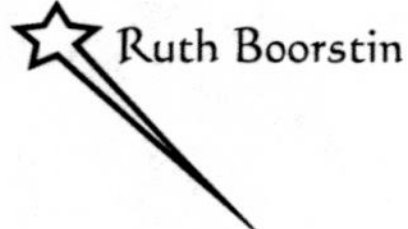

Chapter XIV

Keeping Your Own Space

PAY attention.

If you cannot afford to live by yourself, then you cannot afford to live with *him*. If he cannot afford to live by himself, he has no business living with *you*.

Yes, it is that simple of a decision. Actually, there is no decision to be made if you are in this predicament. Find a friend and share a place. I do not care if you spend most of your nights at your boyfriend's house. Keep your own place until marriage. If you are living together, you are *playing* marriage. You are dating one person, making purchases together, creating a "home"... this is sharing your life with another. This is marriage. Those shacking up are doing the hokey-pokey. They have one foot in and one foot out. What is it going to be in your case? *Are you ready for the commitment or not? Is he?*

Financial assistance is a really weak reason to shack up with a man. The cost to your life is far greater than what you are saving. Women can find themselves in a compromised position. When you move in with a boyfriend, your lives begin to entangle. This means it is harder to break away. Many "false" connections hold you in a situation where you may not belong in the first place. Shacking up with a friend would be a better choice.

Sharing furniture, pets, toothpaste, and the same bed are not the only ingredients in a successful union. And do not give me the, "we have to see if we're compatible" routine. Just open your eyes when you're at his house. Is he clean? Is he sloppy? Could you see yourself living there? That is who he is, and how he likes to live. You wouldn't like a roommate who has opposite living habits from you; why would you want a mate that has opposite living habits? Oh, yeah, I forgot, love conquers all - *not!*

<u>From the National Center for Health Statistics:</u>

1 in 5 marriages
will end in divorce within 5 years

(1 in 2 if they cohabit first!)

1 in 3 marriages
will end in divorce within 10 years

(62% will divorce if they cohabit first!)

Think you can beat the odds?

www.cdc.gov/nchs

For those of you who *think* that shacking up *"works,"* and that it is a positive step towards a lasting marriage, please see the chart to the left.

Living together is desired because we crave companionship. It's nice to have somebody around to share your life with (not to mention the warm body in bed). But, what about the *big time* misunderstanding between the sexes when it comes to shacking up? Many relationship experts say that women tend to expect marriage to be the end result while men see it as a chance to enjoy all the benefits of marriage without being married. Oh, and then there is that "cohabiting avoids the drain of a legal split" excuse. Unless you are engaged and making your wedding plans, living together does not pay off. There is risk and possible fallout to any relationship. So, until you are married, remain focused on the commitment to yourself.

For all of you ***alpha females*** *(intelligent, high achievers and high earners who are dominant in their relationships)*: If your man cannot afford to live by himself, are you prepared to support him for the rest of your life? Do you like having "power" over him? Is your self-esteem so low that you *think* it's the only way he will "love" you? Or, are you betting on his potential?

Remember, it is your choice. Before you choose to support a man through school, career changes, etc., you may want to consider one important fact. It is also important for this man to find his "I AM" before saying "I Do" to any woman. He needs to fulfill a commitment to himself before taking on the responsibilities that go along with being a husband or father. If he cannot stand strong on his own two feet, how is he going to be part of a supportive foundation for marriage and children?

I do not care what society puts forth as acceptable behavior today. Living together is a set-up for failure.

Do you really think you can beat the odds?

☐ I totally get this chapter.
☐ I should re-read this chapter.
☐ __________ (fill in name) needs to read this chapter.

What you want to say on each wedding anniversary:

"I'm blessed to have this wonderful person in my life."

Chapter XV

Down the Road

THIS is the subject that many couples forget to discuss. Maybe they consciously choose NOT to discuss what direction they see their future going *for they know there may be a HUGE disagreement,*
and then their "mate-to-be"
may not want to marry them after all.

Or, they may hear something come out of their loved-one's mouth
that they have been in denial of
(for they want to believe that in time he or she will change).

hmmm . . . not a real strong start to a marriage.

Where do YOU want to be five years down the road? Where do you want to be ten years down the road? A good time to discuss this with your chosen mate is PRIOR to saying "I Do." You are saying "I Do" to sharing a life with this man. **Do you know what he is asking you to share with him and what he will be sharing with you?**

What does marriage mean to you?

How will the finances be handled?

What kind of lifestyle do you desire?

Do you want to start a family?
If so, when?
How many children do you want?
Where do you want to raise this family?
Will one parent stay home with the children?
How do you believe a child should be disciplined?
Will there be spiritual teachings for the children?

"We cannot be a source of strength unless
we nurture our own strength."

M. Scott Peck, Author
The Road Less Traveled
©1978

Only YOU know what is important to discuss so that you can choose a mate that has similar goals.

In 5 years, I look forward to:	**In 5 years, my man looks forward to:**
____________________	____________________
____________________	____________________
____________________	____________________

Do we have a match?

In 10 years, I look forward to:	**In 10 years, my man looks forward to:**
____________________	____________________
____________________	____________________
____________________	____________________

☐ I totally get this chapter.

☐ I should re-read this chapter.

☐ __________ (fill in name) needs to read this chapter.

What each of you value
must be in harmony.

Chapter XVI

Who Cares What You Love About Him

He's cute.
So what.
He's got a great body.
So what.
He drives a nice car.
So what.
He's successful.
So what.

I do not care what you love about your man. In order to avoid the disenchantment many women feel by their third wedding anniversary, you must do the following *(before you start planning your walk down the rose-petaled aisle)*:

Think. Really *think* about the qualities that the man *who would be standing at the end of that aisle* possesses. The good qualities are easy to live with, but what are his "not so wonderful" qualities? Isn't it baffling that we have to be reminded to look at these possible "slow to explode" bombs? Marital bliss is hard to come by when you have once buried bombs eventually exploding in your face. If YOU DECIDE to overlook his characteristics that drive you crazy, make you sad, or cause you to pig out on ice cream, what makes you think that it's going to be any better five years down the road?

Look at each of his "not so wonderful" qualities. Decide if you can live with it AND still sleep well at night when you put your head on the pillow next to his.

For example, a friend "loves" her boyfriend's physical appearance and the fact that he comes from a good family. "His family is loving and he has money," she proclaims. She seems to make excuses for the fact that he lies to her, cheats on her, is lazy, and is terrible in bed. *What woman is getting in line for this man?*

What I love about my guy:	The "not so great" things I overlook, try to make excuses for, or pretend they don't exist:
	this is the "make it" or "break it" column

Hello? How many of you have lost your mind and are making excuses for staying with a man, in spite of the fact that you find his lifestyle preferences irritating?

I am not talking about the fact that your man might never put his coffee cup in the dishwasher or the fact that he insists on washing his car everyday. I am talking about relationship-threatening lifestyle differences.

Don't look away now! We have to come face to face with what we are saying "I Do" to.

Focus on lifestyle preferences.

If you adore everything about your boyfriend, EXCEPT the fact that he chews tobacco, this may be the very thing that breaks the two of you up. *And, no, he will not quit chewing because he loves you.* Do you find his constant spitting attractive? Do you like the way his mouth tastes when he kisses you?

Can you accept the fact that he may chew tobacco for the rest of his life? If you cannot, or will not accept this reality, be smart and choose another mate. Look at your man's lifestyle preferences and compare them REALISTICALLY to yours. Why choose a man that has conflicting preferences to your own?

What each of you value and hold dear must be in harmony.

WHY?

Because it's one less thing to get between the two of you.

When you and your boyfriend disagree, pay close attention to how the two of you handle the situation. Different personalities have different styles of communicating when angry or upset. How a couple "fights" is just as important to the success of a relationship as how a couple "loves."

See him for who he is, not what you want him to be.
This is not about finding a "Mr. Perfect" that doesn't exist.
This book is about finding the "Mr. Perfect for me."

I had a boyfriend who did the week-long "silent treatment" whenever we argued. His communication style (or lack thereof) did not work for me. I would have understood if he had said, "Give me some time to calm down and to think about what I want to say." But my boyfriend was not willing to work on his communication style with me, or a counselor, so I had to move on. It is not only the differences between companions that cause conflict, but also how those differences are handled.

Be aware that there are differences between a man's character and his behaviors. Behaviors can be changed when two people are committed to the relationship, but character is something much more ingrained and not easily or quickly malleable. If a man's character or personality "make-up" turns you off, steer clear of marrying this man -- no matter how good he looks naked.

☐ I totally get this chapter.

☐ I should re-read this chapter.

☐ __________ (fill in name) needs to read this chapter.

"Do you___________
take this man to be your husband,
and accept that his family is
_______________?"

☐ I Do.
And, I'll never complain about ___________.

☐ I cannot.

Chapter XVII

His Family, Your Family

YOU have heard it before. When you marry a man, you also marry his family. Have you met his family? Are you aware of what emotional cues your future mate has picked up from his parents? Are you aware of what emotional actions and reactions you have learned from your mother and father?

What each of you has "learned" from your families (or lack of family) *will* have an affect on how you relate to each other as a couple. Ooh, this is sounding very therapist-like and to keep this book under 184 pages, I cannot get into all the possible scenarios that can put loving bonds or bad blood between siblings and parents.

Do you come from different "cultures?" Not necessarily different countries, but do the two of you come from different cultural environments? How will this affect your relationship? Was his mother divorced three times and are your parents still married? Does that affect the way that you each view marriage and divorce? This is about *your particular situation*, and you must take notice of what factor(s) you like *and dislike* about his family.

The question is: will you be okay with those factors until death do you part? When you say "I Do" to your man, you are also saying "I do accept your family as they are."

Let's say the man in your life is very close to his mother (this could also be his father, brother, or sister). You happen to find her overbearing, opinionated, and rude. This WILL BE an issue. You can only smile with your teeth clenched for so long. Then you will erupt like a long-over-due volcano. YOU married this man, knowing FULL WELL that his mother irritates you. And, do not give him the "you have to make a choice; it's me or your mother" ultimatum.

"If we would allow giving up of
the effects of previous conditionings
and become able again to experience -
even unfold, our untapped potential,
only then would we live normally -
according to our actual human design -
which has rich possibilities ... for ..."

Elsa Gindler

My guess is that he knows all about what his mother is or is not. We are given our families, but how lucky we are to be able to CHOOSE our mates. Who wants to get married to be miserable at every holiday gathering?

Hopefully, you will choose a man who will remember that you are now his family too.

- ☐ I totally get this chapter.
- ☐ I should re-read this chapter.
- ☐ ___________ (fill in name) needs to read this chapter.

♪

"And you can't fix a man when he's wrong!"

Rodgers & Hammerstein

Chapter XVIII
Damaged and Irregular Goods

OKAY, so the title of this chapter is a little harsh.

Damaged Goods are men with serious addictions that often lead to abusive behavior. Irregular Goods are the men with major character flaws, such as narcissism and selfishness. If you desire a safe and supportive environment, why would you cuddle up with one of these relationship time bombs?

Why make sappy excuses for staying with a man who has a major addiction or character flaw?

"Because I love him."
"Because no one else will love me."
"Because he is going to change."
Or, maybe, it is because you have no courage, faith, or self-esteem to move on to better quality goods.

Do you want children? I would think you would want a great man to be the father of your child. Your choice will be affecting future generations.

The Druggie -
When the father of your child starts hiding drugs in the diaper bag, maybe you will wake up. Maybe not. Those people who suffer from an addiction put that addiction **above all.** (Yes, this includes family, a girlfriend, wife, and children.) Their priority in life is feeding that addiction. Responsibility beyond that will not be one of their strong qualities.

I have a close friend who attends AL-ANON (support groups for friends and family members of addicts) meetings, for she chose to have a child with a recovering drug addict, who just happens to fall off the wagon from time to time.

"No man should ever hit a woman,
for he has to go to sleep some time and then
he'd have a large frying pan smashed on his head."

My Mom

> *Is my friend's boyfriend cute?*
> Yes.
> *Funny?*
> Yes.
> *Is she sexually attracted to him?*
> Yes.
> *Does he care for their child?*
> He will take part in his son's life when *his* life is not compromised.

If you are "in love" with some type of addict, go sit in on a few AL-ANON meetings and **<u>see if it is where you want to be in the future.</u>**

The Abuser -
In Chapter VIII, we talk about roles. If the role of "punching bag" is your current situation, you are in bigger trouble than this book was meant to handle.

Men that bully women or children are pitiful human beings. Real men who are in check with their self-esteem, ego, pride, self-worth, *and* possess a loving disposition, will come to the aid of those that are weaker than themselves. They **absolutely** NEVER intentionally harm another human being, unless out of self-defense or defense of another.

Please see a counselor to get help with a situation that can have a deadly ending.

The Drinker -
There's the functioning alcoholic that drinks five vodka tonics after work each night and then there is the angry alcoholic that erupts into violent behavior. Neither is a smart choice. (Try for door number three.) Again, go to a few AL-ANON meetings and **<u>see if this is where you want to be in the future.</u>**

Those people who suffer from an addiction
put that addiction **above all.**

The Attention Addicts -

These are the narcissistic, selfish men that qualify as Irregular Goods. Narcissistic men need TONS of CONSTANT attention. These men are are addicted to adoration. The adoration required to keep them happy is exhausting.

I knew a woman who had such a husband. Many times throughout the day she "had to" tell him how great he was or "how great" something he did was, all to feed his self-obsessive nature. (My mother and father have been married for over 40 years, and my mother does not have to feed my Dad's ego every hour on the hour.)

A friend of mine chose to marry an attention junkie. He gets visibly upset if she or one of their two children takes away from him being "worshiped" by others. She herself is starved for attention, because he gives her none. *(Notice that attention junkies are very competitive when it comes to someone stealing attention away from them.)* The "attention competition" that occurs between my friend and her husband is a sad thing to watch.

I was lucky enough to date one of the most selfish men on this planet. Why do I consider myself lucky? That relationship showed me exactly what (bad) quality I **do not want** in a man. What is attractive about life-sucking men anyway? Selfish men drain the life right out of you. Many divorced men seem to possess this talent. (Maybe they have it in their heads that they "gave sooooooo much" in their prior marriage, that they now need to look out for number one.)

Beware… if it's all about HIS schedule, HIS desires, HIS needs, HIS wants, HIS responsibilities to everything in the universe but you . . . run for your life.

*Wouldn't it be wonderful if love
could cure someone's addictive behaviors?*

This type of man does not understand that reciprocity is the fuel in a supportive relationship. He will only worry about his own tank; therefore, expect yours to be constantly drained. (See Chapter XIII, *Reciprocity.*)

Why consciously choose a man who is damaged goods or irregular goods? Do you consider yourself damaged goods and that this is all you deserve? Or are you pretending that love conquers all and his addiction problems or life-sucking behaviors are no big deal? It's your life, your choice.

☐ I totally get this chapter.
☐ I should re-read this chapter.
☐ __________ (fill in name) needs to read this chapter.

"The actions of men are the best
interpreters of their thoughts."

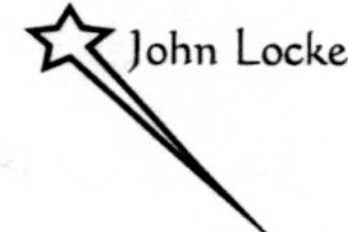

John Locke

Chapter IX

The Trust Factor

LEARN this right now.
When you talk to men, you must be extremely specific.

Asking a question such as, *"Is there something I should know?"* is not going to get you any information about a situation that is nudging at your sixth sense. If you surmise something about your boyfriend, you must hit with a direct, detailed, leaves-nothing-to-the-imagination-loophole line of questioning. ***Why?*** Because some people feel that omission is not a lie. Some people will only answer exactly what they are asked. For example, *"Did you sleep with another woman?"* can easily be answered, "No." It needs to be, *"Did any other woman, besides me, have any type of physical contact with you? I am not worried about the sleeping part - it's the kissing, oral sex, or possible intercourse that I am referring to. Whether you did it in a bed, on the floor, in your car, or in a different area code does not make it any less trivial. Now, is 'No' still your final answer?"*

Do you know or do you think you know? Remember to protect yourself and your future. How well do you really know the man you are dating and thinking of marrying? Ask questions. If he has nothing to hide, he should be able to simply answer any questions you may have. I know that it will be hard for some of you to enter into this territory.

You love him; shouldn't you trust him completely?

Not yet. Please do not play the, "I don't want to hear about his past. It's *our future* that is important and he loves me." You are right; it is *your future* that is important. Isn't your future worth asking *the person you love* some questions that may make you temporarily uncomfortable?

What are YOU telling
(or not telling)
your man?

Many smart women have fallen in love and married a man that was still married to someone else, or had children that he never spoke of, or was using an alias (not his real name), or had a history of marriages that ended because of infidelity. I ask you again - ***Do you really know your man?*** If necessary, hire a private detective to verify his story and to ease your mind.

If any type of distrust exists, ask yourself, "Why am I choosing to have this man be a part of my life?" [I hope] you do not keep untrustworthy friends around, so why keep an untrustworthy man around? Healthy choices lead to healthy relationships which result in a happy heart.

Remember, trust is earned, not automatically given just because you are excited about being part of a couple. To love honestly and be honestly loved back is the goal. Those looking to take advantage of "love" do not have "Don't Trust Me" tattooed on their foreheads. Be careful of who you allow into your life and into your heart.

☐ I totally get this chapter.
☐ I should re-read this chapter.
☐ __________ (fill in name) needs to read this chapter.

Adore the men that are enamored by women.

Chapter XX
Wimps & Liars

Chutzpah. (Yiddish)
Cojones. (Spanish)
Quioni. (Italian)
Balls. (American)
This chapter is about those men who are challenged in this area.

These are the "I really only care about myself" men that will say and do anything to bring about their own pleasure. Well, life's cruel trick on us is this: these are also the same men we will be attracted to because of their good looks, sexual magnetism, charming manner, and that exciting "live-for-the-moment" persona.

These men can only offer you little moments. They are usually married, divorced, workaholics, or have every other thing in the universe going on that needs their attention.

A wimp is extremely good with the excuses of why you are not number one in his life. Hopefully, if you are in this situation now, you will tire of it real soon and make *yourself* number one. Sometimes you have to clean out your "closet" in order to clear space for better possibilities to find their way into your life. If you fall for one of these selfish individuals, you will eventually realize that they have very little to offer in terms of love, companionship, and honesty.

These men have no balls - *oh, I'm sorry* - I meant morals. (Slip of the tongue.) Wimps have no backbone or regard for women in a loving relationship. They lie to women, their friends, themselves, and anyone who is about to put a damper on their self-satisfying actions.

We need to love the opposite of these men. Adore the men that are enamored by women.

I cannot change him.
I cannot change him.
I cannot change him.

I can choose a better man.

There is nothing more attractive in a man than his desire to make a woman an *integral* part of his life (not some distraction that is there for his sole pleasure). I often wonder what type of relationship Wimps have with their mother, and what type of relationship a Wimp's parents displayed during important childhood years when the impressionable brain was storing the unconscious thoughts that affect adult decisions. (There are also plenty of good psychology books out there if you want to dig deeper into the marvels of childhood issues.)

Girls, be on the lookout for the Wimps, who for some reason capture your heart. These men can only do one thing to your heart: break it. They do not have the capacity to be in a loving relationship. (The loving relationship they have with themselves does not count.) And no, you are not the "wonder woman" who will change him "this time." Let me repeat that: no, you are not the "wonder woman" who will change him "this time." *If you have trouble convincing yourself of this,* scribble on the bathroom mirror with a dry erase marker or tube of lipstick, "I cannot change him. I am worth more than what he has to offer." (℞ Read 2X daily as you brush your teeth.)

☐ I totally get this chapter.
☐ I should re-read this chapter.
☐ __________ (fill in name) needs to read this chapter.

"People call me a feminist whenever I express sentiments that differentiate me from a doormat or a prostitute."

Rebecca West

Chapter XXI

MCPs

IS an MCP for you? Do you really know what one is? MCPs come in many shapes and sizes. They could be 23, 35, or 47 years old. They could be life insurance consultants, mortgage brokers, or even close relatives.

Let's break it down.

> **Male** adj. - referring to men/boys
> **Chauvinist** n. - person who believes that one gender is superior over another
> **Pig**[headed] adj.inf. - obstinate

Simplified - a man who will not change his mind about his belief that males are superior to females. ***Ewww!***

These men have not yet figured out how incredible women truly are. They surround themselves with women who they can "save," teach, have power over, or intimidate in some way. They actually cannot conceive the notion that women can be intelligent, and heaven forbid, capable of doing something better than a man. Who raised these ignoramuses?

If you choose to marry an MCP, you are saying "I Do" to a man who believes that women are the dumber, weaker sex that needs to be "led." He is not *all of a sudden* going to realize how amazing YOU ARE and then change his view of world order.

Girls, remember that what you decide to represent in this world also sends a message to men of what all women represent. *What do you represent?* Are you the MCP's generic bikini chick? What type of woman is striving to be the girl that stands in a bikini next to the guy that only wants her standing beside him *because* she is in a bikini? (Maybe we need to go back and read the Self-Worth Chapter.)

Why set yourself up for a lifetime of
jumping from lily pad to lily pad
kissing whom you hope may turn out to be a Prince Charming?

But, hey,
if being the bikini chick
standing next to the guy
who wants a bikini chick standing next to him
is your goal *and makes you happy*,
you go girl.

*No complaining in the future that he does not appreciate you beyond the fact that you look good in a bikini. Remember? That is what brought the two of you together in the first place. Is that the role you are going to be content to fill forever? (See Chapter VIII, *What Role Are You Auditioning For?*)

In healthy relationships, males and females learn from one another. They enhance each other's lives. They each believe that the other adds something vital to their life together.

If your current *need* is to be "led," or taught, or flaunted, or taken care of, I suggest that you learn how to swim on your own.

☐ I totally get this chapter.
☐ I should re-read this chapter.
☐ __________ (fill in name) needs to read this chapter.

♪

"Isn't happiness worth more
than a gold or diamond ring?"

☆ performed by Savage Garden

Chapter XXII

Baggage Weigh-In

THIS chapter is very important for all of you women who do not like to be treated like coleslaw.

Coleslaw is a side dish. The free *side* or free *extra* that comes with a *main* meal. If you enjoy being a side dish and not the main course, then by all means go ahead and hook up with a man that has tons of "baggage." "Baggage" that came before you, "baggage" that needs attention, "baggage" that will take away from your time together, and "baggage" that will foster arguments between the two of you that have absolutely NOTHING TO DO WITH YOU.

Once again, you must decide what role you want to play in your man's life.

You will need to "weigh" his baggage by deciding if the time he spends with you is fulfilling and allows for the nurturing of your relationship. Is the time you spend together quality time? There are only so many hours in a day - *24 to be exact* - and if you take away the time for sleeping, working, showering, eating, and probably some type of hobby if he is a healthy man - the remaining time would be with YOU. (BIG GASP) But oh, he has to visit with his children (if he is a good father), he has to collaborate schedules with his ex-wife(s), and he may possibly need some time to be by himself (to calm down after being annoyed by the ex-wife, who is still angry that her fairytale marriage did not end in happily-ever-after).

His ex-wife (or ex-wives) can play a BIG part in determining what percentage of time the two of you (do or don't) have to share. (Believe it!) Are you okay with that? Are you okay with the fact that there will be times that his responsibilities will take him away from his time with you? This could include holidays or events that are important to you and your family/friends.

What is impacting your relationship?

Another aspect to consider is what elements in your life have to blend with his. Do you have children? Do you have an ex-husband or an ex-boyfriend who will impact this new relationship?

Divorce is hard on all those involved. In order to have harmony in your relationship, you will have to create strategies to cope with the new situations.

The "simplest" type of relationship is when you have a girl and a boy who come together with no other forces affecting the interchanges of this new union.

The only reason the word "simplest" was used is because any other relationship that includes an ex-wife (or ex-wives) and children will be much more complicated. If no strategies are discussed to handle the other forces impacting a new union, the couple is setting themselves up for failure. How odd that a relationship that is still new will warrant the boy and girl to consider each other's needs when it comes to dealing with the "baggage."

Remember, we cannot help whom we fall in love with, but we can choose whom we marry.

Part of the baggage that must be weighed is your boyfriend's point of reference in regard to relationships. *Is it complementary to yours?*

> *Does he come from a divorced family life? If so, how has this impacted his idea of marriage?*
>
> *Do you come from a divorced family life? How has this impacted your idea of marriage?*

Sometimes, the broken roads we have traveled
inspire us to make better future decisions.

Other times, we sadly allow those broken roads
to dictate our future, as if we're powerless.

If a fabulous man comes into your life, you must also be able to say "I Do" to ALL of the baggage that he brings with him when you say "I Do" to him on your wedding day.

Sadly, 2nd and 3rd marriages involving children have a very high rate of divorce (the exact percentage depends upon the study and factors). Remarried couples are often faced with conflict between a stepparent and stepchild and that can be enough to threaten the stability of the marriage.

More power to you if you are in this situation *and for the sake of those children that have already endured divorce*, my strength is with you and your future husband.

☐ I totally get this chapter.

☐ I should re-read this chapter.

☐ __________ (fill in name) needs to read this chapter.

The one question to ask yourself
when you're thinking of getting back together
with him -

"What's going to be different this time?"

Chapter XXIII

On Again, Off Again

Here is a real set-up for marriage failure -- the ever popular, *On Again-Off Again Relationship.*

This is a **short chapter to reflect the length of time your marriage will last if you marry Mister "I'm not your complementary match, but we'll stay together because we're too freaked out by the thought of having to go back out into the dating world."*

If your current relationship can be described as

on again
off again
on again
off again...

What makes you think your marriage won't be too? Oh yeah, I forgot (ha ha ha), the pixie dust at the ceremony that changes *everything*. Your man puts on a tuxedo, says the words "I Do," and magically becomes the complementary match for you that he never was before.

This would actually be funny if there were not so many women who believed it to be true.

But wait . . . there is hope - even if you are in this situation now.

4 stages of growth are needed.

1- Find the courage to cut the cord that connects you to the unhealthy boyfriend. (Chapter XXIV, *No One Else Will Love Me*)

2- Brave being single long enough to figure out what YOU are all about. (Chapter II, *Self-Worth*)

♪

"Sometimes we're meant to stay,
Sometimes we're meant to go."

☆ performed by Jessica Andrews

3- Make a vow to yourself that you "deserve to find the lid that fits your pot." (Chapter XI, *The BIG Four*)

4- Stay open-minded as to "what" or "who" may be your complementary match. Take note of all the new experiences you will have - even the uncomfortable ones! They may be the most meaningful in order for you to move toward a healthy relationship! (Chapter III, *Get Past the Old and Familiar*)

No matter what feelings of loneliness, longing, horniness, or desire may pull on your heartstrings and weaken your reasoning for moving on to a better relationship, stay true to yourself and KNOW that you do have a choice when it comes to the happiness or sadness of your future. Oh, and by the way, you WILL get over this guy. As I always say, "This too shall pass."

☐ I totally get this chapter.
☐ I should re-read this chapter.
☐ ___________ (fill in name) needs to read this chapter.

"Sometimes you have to follow your dreams
without compromising for others."

Karen Flynn Snyder

Chapter XXIV

"No One Else Will Love Me"

FOR all of you who have trouble letting go and moving on, this chapter is for you.

How fast we get attached to men. *Would your family and friends say you act as if you are covered in Velcro?* Even some of the strongest, most independent women I know have quickly become attached to the emotional whirl of a new relationship. But, it's the settling into the comfort phase and not wanting to be back out in the dating world that will be the focus of this chapter.

How many girlfriends do you have that constantly complain about their boyfriends? They complain about what he does or does not do as if they are stuck with him! Why spend time with someone that makes you miserable? This is where dating pays off. You get to spend time with a guy to see if he is someone that adds beauty to your life. Take off the crown that you think is atop your head that lets the world know, "I'm special because I have a boyfriend." You might have a boyfriend, but is he in harmony with you?

Good-byes are hard, but sometimes necessary.

I know it's hard. I know it's hard to let go of whatever it is about your guy that you do love. It's going to hurt. A relationship is a living entity. Moving on will cause a death--a death of that living entity. You will miss the person you talk to everyday. You will miss your "best friend" that has been a big part of your life. You will not "belong" to anyone except yourself. After being part of a couple for a long time, that can be scary.

The longer you are in a relationship, the harder it is to drum up the courage to move on. FEAR. It can hold you in neutral gear for years.

♪

"He doesn't treat you right,
but you hold on so tight.
Is it really better than nothing?"

performed by The Braxton Brothers

Are you going to let being uncomfortable in a so-called comfortable situation get in your way of actually finding a harmonious relationship? Any negative, self-deflating thoughts need to be thrown out the window. What you put out to the world is what you will attract. Think about that last statement for a minute. What are you putting out to the world? *"I'm a woman who wants a fabulous man"* . . . or . . . *"I'm a woman that will take anything she can get."*

You will be okay - I promise. If you find the balls to look at *who you are* and *who would be compatible with you*, you will no longer stay in "comfortable" relationships (that really aren't so comfortable). Aligning yourself with a compatible man is a better bet for lifelong happiness than the haphazard coupling that is preceding marriages of today (the same marriages that have a 62% chance of divorce).

Have faith in your journey.
Is it time to move on?

Sure enough, another man will come along to affect your life somehow. How many new men will you be open to meeting? <u>There will always be another man who will fall in love with you</u>, no matter how much weight you have gained, or that you recently lost your job, or that your hair stylist screwed up the last time you had your hair cut. Open your heart, open your mind, and most importantly, focus on what YOU are looking for in a partner.

> If a man wants to break-up with you or walks out of your life because a commitment to you and to the relationship is too overwhelming, let him go. Did you ever think that this is not the man for you? Maybe, just maybe, because you have not had the courage to move on, other forces are working to put you in a better place. A fearless, intelligent, open-eyed, experienced, confident, loving, and lovable woman does not hold onto an unhealthy relationship.

"If I'd have known the way that this would end,
If I'd have read the last page first,
If I'd have had the strength to walk away,
If I'd have known how this would hurt,
I would have loved you anyway,
I'd do it all the same,
Not a second I would change,
Not a touch that I would trade,
Had I known my heart would break,
I'd have loved you anyway."

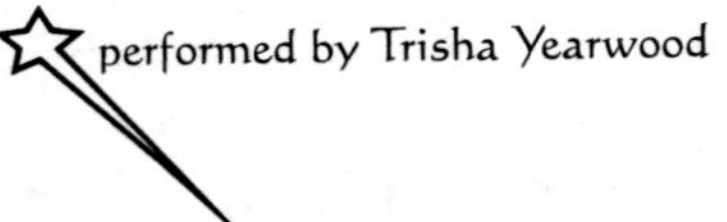

Remember to ***love & learn.***

Love is not - wanting to be with someone just to be with someone.
Love is not - wanting to be with someone because you're horny.
Love is not - wanting to be with someone to feel secure.

Love is - truly discovered when two devoted individuals have come together to make each other's life the most amazing joyride possible.

☐ I totally get this chapter.
☐ I should re-read this chapter.
☐ __________ (fill in name) needs to read this chapter.

SHERMAN'S LAGOON
BY J.P. TOOMEY
A DOZEN LONG-STEMS... WHERE WOULD YOU LIKE THEM?
OVER THERE.
TELL HIM TO GET MORE CHOCOLATES. AND NO MORE OF THIS CHEAP STUFF. I WANT GODIVAS.
RIGHT AWAY.
PLAY SOMETHING UPBEAT.
YES, MA'AM.
SHOWTIME!
YOU'RE ON.
MAN, I HATE MATING SEASON.

Chapter XXV

"Treat Me Like the Goddess That I Am"

ARETHA Franklin couldn't have said it any better . . .

R - E - S - P - E - C - T

Respect is what I see the least of in today's couples. The lack of this essential relationship ingredient is at the root of many "irreconcilable differences."

When you say "I Do" to each other, you have made a decision (hopefully a wise one) to put your faith, hope, love, and commitment into this ONE person. This *chosen* man now gets to fill the shoes of the men that adored, loved, cherished, befriended, and uplifted your soul *before he became your spouse*. This one man has taken a vow to do his part to make you feel admired, adored, sexy, pretty, horny, and happy. He is your partner. Remember? He will be 50% of your happiness and sadness from this point forward. *Can he fill this position? What are you setting yourself up for?*

While it may be important to you to retain friendships with other men, it will be unhealthy to your marriage if these friendships are *meant to take the place of* a missing quality in YOUR man. *Ouch*--that hurts. I've been there and definitely done that - wishing I could combine the positive attributes of three men into one. This is what I call "The Cauldron Syndrome." Wouldn't it be great if we could take the best qualities of three different men, put them in a pot, and stir them together for our "Mr. Perfect?" *mmm, mmm, good.*

Not that we are "perfect," but, ***wow, women are amazing creatures.***

Any man who does not think enough of you to "worship the ground you hover over" is NOT WORTHY of your life-long love, care, friendship, sexual pleasures, emotional support, and so on. PUT YOUR ENERGY where it is deserved and appreciated!

"Oh, the many hotel lounges I have sat in during my travels
only to be approached by some ringless married man
downplaying his marital life.

Note to self,
I've got to get that neon sign removed from my forehead that says,
'If you disrespect women and have no integrity, talk to me.'"

Does your man love you
whether you are 118 lbs, 169 lbs, or ____lbs?

Does your man make you feel like
you are the most beautiful woman in the world?

Is he genuinely interested in YOU? Or, does he have "roving eyes" when out in public? Is that not the ultimate in disrespect -- when the man sitting across from you is "oogling" every girl that walks by? Where did gentlemanly manners go? Mothers: Teach your sons the etiquette of holding the door open for a woman, walking on the outside of the sidewalk, and letting her order her meal first. Let him know that everyone wins when he makes his partner #1.

If you cannot hold a man's attention BEFORE you get married, do not expect to hold it after you are married. **There is no fairy dust at the wedding ceremony that transforms your man into an adoring husband when he never had an ounce of adoration in him to begin with.**

"The First Two Months Don't Count" (Chapter VI) reminds us that we need to be courted for the rest of our lives, not just for the first 60-days of the relationship. Sometimes guys are so tacky that they only act attentive until they have finagled their way into getting you horizontal. Let us not forget that it is *us* who determines when sex will take place. So, if you want it, go for it, but do not be upset when the guy who does not respect women will no longer be attentive once he has "scored" with you. These types of guys WILL NEVER CHANGE. Do not take their disregard personally. They just don't get it. These self-centered egotistical creatures are the opposite of the fabulous mate you deserve. We all know those women that make sappy excuses about why they stay with a man who is missing the portion of the brain that enables him to love, honor, and cherish her. Who cares about how gorgeous his eyes are, how hard it would be to date again, how you own a house together, how his family is "now like your family," . . . when the bottom line is that he treats you like _ _ _ _.

goddess *n.* a woman of great beauty or grace

Zero in on the way your man views women in general. This is the way he will eventually view you over time. *How does he treat his mother? Is he respectful to waitresses? Does he frequent strip bars? Ooh - you know there is no way I can write a book about personal relationships and not include the topic of strip bars.*

It amuses me how advocates of places that boast "Totally Live Nudes" believe that they are empowering women. (Yeah, right. I am still confused as to why this is referred to as "Gentlemen's Entertainment." "Gentlemen" I know do not frequent such establishments.)

When I saw for myself how each "dancer" had to shake her T&A in skanky guys' faces, *and then crawl around on the floor picking up $1 tips,* it never entered my mind that this was somehow empowering to women.

Girlfriend, do not kid yourself. If your man views women as sexual objects, domestic servants, or anything less than the goddesses that they truly are, kick him further than the curb - kick him out of your world. Surround yourself with people who hold you in high regard. **Marry a man who holds you in high regard.**

My girlfriend is unhappily married to a man who constantly tells her that she should get a breast enhancement so that he could be sexually attracted to her. (I couldn't kick off my high heels fast enough to run away from this prize.) She chose a man who would rather look at the *near-naked chic magazine that happens to be popular at the moment* than make love to her.

You each need to decide what is important for holding your marriage bond together.

"Coming around you may wake up to find,
Questions deep within your eyes,
Things you never realized."

performed by Van Halen

For my girlfriend's husband, it is big boobs. Why he chose a small-breasted woman, I do not know. (I guess he'll have to read my next book for men!) My girlfriend was aware that he always looked at big-breasted women BEFORE they were married. Now she wishes that she had questioned this and avoided marrying a man that would never find her body attractive.

After years of living with his negativity, she has a terrible self/body image and basically feels "stuck" in a marriage where she will endlessly try to get the approval of a man who is not worthy of receiving two percent of her attention. She has a child with this "man" and, therefore, feels divorce would be a bitter pill to swallow. Who wants to be in her situation? Any hands raised?

Pay attention to what turns each of you on--mind, body, and soul. Remember that what turns you on at 21 may drastically change at 29. Develop yourself into a goddess first, and then seek out "the lid that fits your pot." Be sure that the man YOU CHOOSE respects you and above all . . .

Respect yourself - today, tomorrow, always.

- ☐ I totally get this chapter.
- ☐ I should re-read this chapter.
- ☐ __________ (fill in name) needs to read this chapter.

"After a while, you learn the subtle difference
Between holding a hand and chaining a soul.
And you learn that love doesn't mean possession
And company doesn't mean security,
And loneliness is universal.
And you learn that kisses aren't contracts,
And presents aren't promises...
And you begin to accept your defeats
With your head up and your eyes open,
With the grace of a woman, not the grief of a child.
And you learn to build all of your hope on today,
Because tomorrow's ground is too uncertain,
And futures have a way of falling down in mid-flight
Because tomorrow's ground can be too uncertain for plans;
Yet each step taken in a new direction creates a path
Towards the promise of a brighter dawn.
After a while you learn that even sunshine burns
If you get too much.

So you plant your own garden,
And nourish your own soul
Instead of waiting for someone to bring you flowers.
And you learn that you really can endure...
That you really are strong,
And you really do have worth.
And you learn and grow...
With every good-bye you learn."

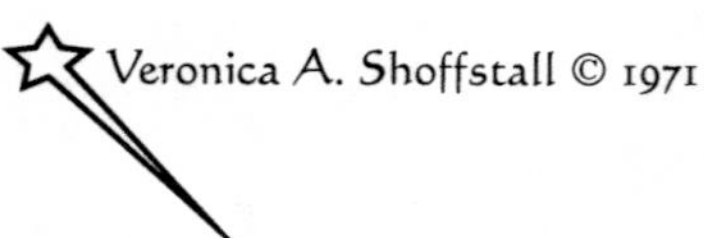
Veronica A. Shoffstall © 1971

Chapter XXVI

Be the Last One of Your Girlfriends to Get Married

WE cannot help whom we fall in love with, and yes, you will love many men.

We can choose whom we marry.

Think of all your family and friends who are married. Did they make wise choices? If you wrote down each couple's names on a piece of paper, how would you rate their marriage on a scale of 1-10? What factors are you looking at to determine this rating? You are probably looking at the factors that are most important to you. Were there more fives or nines in your ratings?

Did your friends marry at a healthy stage in their life's journey?

Did your friends marry for convenience?

Did they marry out of desperation or co-dependence?

Did they marry their best friend?

Does the couple emotionally support one another?

Did they marry an incredible man or a "loser"?

Did they marry on the rebound from a failed relationship?

Do their families get along?

What contributed to any failed marriages?

How long did they date?

"Life is too short to not learn from other people's mistakes."

What are the joys and hardships that your family and friends are experiencing because of their choices?

____

____

____

Learn from your friends' successes and failures. When they chose, were they just in love with the concept of love? Were they in a big hurry to flaunt a diamond ring, wear a beautiful dress, and be queen for a day? If you need to - buy yourself a gorgeous ring, spend a day trying on beautiful dresses, throw yourself a party, and go on a trip . . . this way when the honeymoon ends, you will still belong to you. Be patient with your journey. When you choose your mate, be in love with the man you marry for all the right reasons, NOT because you are in love with the concept of love or because it is what everyone else is doing.

Amid the many divorced couples and broken families of today, it is wonderful to personally know couples and families that are healthy and thriving. I am proud to have some family and friends that are good examples of happy unions. These men and women looked at the reality of their situations before saying "I Do."

LOVE

A second marriage for a friend meant more than great shared adventures with her boyfriend. When she said "I Do," she understood that her new husband longed for his own son or daughter. She would have another baby, and he would love her child from a previous marriage as his own.

LOVE

Another friend had to decide whether or not she wanted a baby. Her would-be husband was content with the one child from a previous marriage. The two truly injected love into each other's lives, but she had to make this decision for herself, knowing that he was not going to change his mind.

A good marriage is -
being able to say,
"You double my joy and divide my grief."

Imagine marrying the wrong guy. A friend almost did because she was in a big hurry to find a husband before turning 30. She pulled back from what would have been a set-up for failure and then found the right guy. This loving man and my friend now have two adorable children. They did it "right" the first time around!

LOVE

They say to marry your best friend. My friend did and in doing so said "I Do" to his three children and ex-wife from a previous marriage. As this is the second time around for the both of them, they have learned the importance of being each other's support system.

LOVE

I have aunts and uncles that still laugh at each other's quirks and enjoy each other's company. They are solid foundations for their children and are representative of what marriage truly is - a commitment to oneself, to the chosen partner, and to family.

☐ I totally get this chapter.
☐ I should re-read this chapter.
☐ ___________ (fill in name) needs to read this chapter.

"Somebody told me love makes you stupid,
Makes you go crazy, Makes you go blind,
Comes uninvited and leaves when it wants to,
Calls you at midnight and ties up your line,
But it's oh so sweet when it's right, There's nothing better,
And you swear you won't but you might,
You're gonna try,
Gotta fumble in the dark, If you wanna see the light."

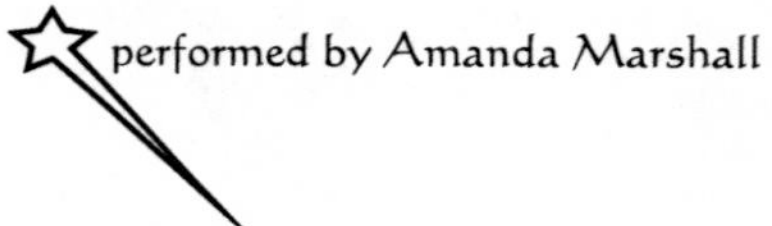
performed by Amanda Marshall

Chapter XXVII

The Natural Order of Things

TO all you older than 20-something chickadees -
Do you continually lay down the carpet before you paint the walls? Just as there is a natural order to redecorating a home, there is a natural order to personal growth.

I did not make up this order. It is just the way it is.

You can accept it and finally identify who you are and who would make a fabulous mate for you

or

you can continue to sabotage your chance of having a successful relationship, as you haphazardly accept any man that happens to be in your life at the moment. You may be the best thing that came into his life, BUT is he the best thing to come into your life? (Of course we never think about this until we are past the tears and heartache of coming to terms with another "it didn't work out" relationship.)

A reason, a season, or a lifetime - men will be in your life for one of these three.

As a fearless, intelligent, open-eyed, experienced, confident, loving, and lovable woman - I ask you - isn't it time you paint the walls before laying down the carpet?

Stop thinking that every man you date could be "the one." Go out with men to figure out what characteristics you will want in a fabulous mate. (I know how you all rationalize a man's marriage potential. Well, no more rationalizing about the very aspect of him that will drive you to divorce.) That is Step One - to figure out what you like and do not like in a companion. Sounds simple, no?

What are you commiting yourself to?

- ☐ a set-up for failure
- ☐ a set-up for success

Then why is it that so many of you go directly to the "I think he could be the one, because we totally connected at dinner the other night?" So you had a great time at dinner. He's fun. Can we go through the rest of the necessary steps please? Then when the carpet is laid it stays beautiful - not ruined by all the stripping, sanding, and painting you will be doing.

So, let's get this down to memory.

Strip the old paint. Look inside yourself to realize what you want in a fabulous mate. Face who you truly are and what you want out of life. This is the time to decide whether you want an adoring husband with a house in the 'burbs, an absentee husband who works round the clock leaving you in the city condo alone, a man who sets you up in a trailer park where it's convenient for him to cheat on you with his cousin, or a combination of these (I do not want to get yelled at for being stereotypical). Remember, there are no rules, only choices. I am not here to judge your choices, only to remind you to take self-responsibility for the choices you make. (I am hoping that you will make better choices after reading this book. You now have an advantage that I did not have, so no excuses!)

Sand the walls. Refine your wants by dating men (not just "hanging out" and "hooking up") to be sure you can recognize a good guy vs. a bad guy for YOU to marry. **This does not mean he is a bad guy, just a bad choice for a fabulous mate.** Maybe he is somebody else's fabulous mate. Remember, there is a lid to fit every pot. (See Chapter XI, *The Big Four*.)

Paint the walls. Color your world with the thought that you are a fearless, intelligent, open-eyed, experienced, confident, loving, and lovable woman. Smile, walk, and live each day as the goddess you truly are. *Hold that head high!*

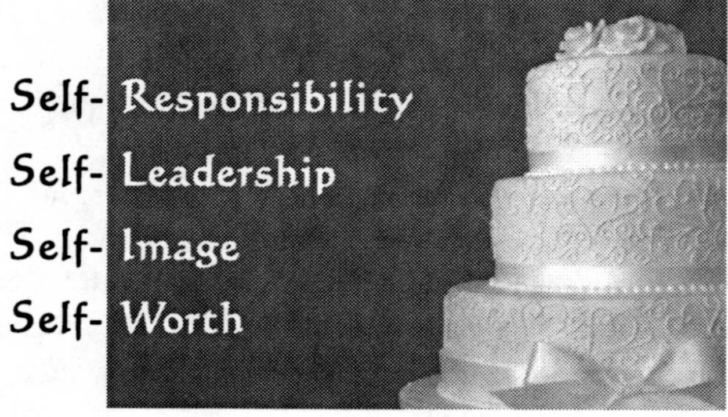
Self- Responsibility
Self- Leadership
Self- Image
Self- Worth

Lay down the matting. Choose a mate that provides good cushioning and can go the distance. (Avoid those cheap ones that wear out after only a couple of years.)

Lay the new carpet. When the time is right and the man is right, get married! Yes, go for it with the confidence that you took the time to wisely choose a fabulous mate. *Congratulations!*

☐ I totally get this chapter.

☐ I should re-read this chapter.

☐ __________ (fill in name) needs to read this chapter.

*No matter what your thoughts are on evolution,
this quotation has the right message.*

"Woman was created from the rib of man.
She was not made from his head to top him,
Nor out of his feet to be trampled upon.
But, out of his side, to be equal to him, to be protected,
And, near his heart, to be loved."

Ranee A. Spina
Author/Speaker

AFTER spending fifteen years in the marketing and advertising industry writing about other people, it is very difficult to turn the spotlight on myself. Many readers profess their interest in the "where I came from" and "why I do what I do." So, as not to have to repeat myself, here are the basics.

As a little girl, I would play out in front of my house in Broomall, PA (a suburb of Philadelphia). As I sang *Rain Drops Keep Falling on My Head* to an imaginary audience in the street, I had a thought about my life as a "grown-up." I told my mother, "You have to become famous before you get married." To me, "famous" meant to be successful. (As a little girl I probably did not know the word "successful" yet.) My understanding at that young age was that I had to become something in my own right before I got married. That is where my philosophy on life started - I kid you not.

I was lucky to have lived next to a very talented dance teacher who taught me how to be an entertainer. I went on to New York University at age seventeen to study Business for my Father and to study dance, singing, and acting to fulfill my own dreams.

At age nineteen, I moved to Los Angeles to be discovered, but did not have the confidence to go to an audition. I ended up doing wardrobe, staging, and merchandising for many of the big hair bands of the 80's. (Those guys were so jealous of my big hair!)

The Corporate Identity world attracted me, and I immersed myself in the design of Branded Marketing Communications. After twelve years on the rollercoaster ride of matching businesses with their target markets, I knew that there was something else for me to do.

Ranee A. Spina
Author/Speaker

One day, while in the beautiful bathtub of my rented guesthouse, the idea for this book hit me. I jumped out of the tub and wrote down twenty-five of the chapter titles that appear on these pages. Relationship Java Nights at a coffee house led to TV and radio interviews, which led to speaking engagements. The feedback from audiences thanking me for inspiring them to live their lives a little bit differently is why I do what I do.

My audiences have also inspired me. I am back in school looking forward to a PhD in Social Psychology. No, I do not want to be a therapist. I just want to write books and stand on stage and make people laugh about their choices when it comes to love.

Here I am, thirty years later becoming that something I was put here to do. I finally had the courage and took the time to find my “I AM.”

This triumph is dedicated to Faith.
Faith in being able to get out of bed
when all you want to do is close your eyes
and never wake up again,
Faith in getting up each time something
or someone knocks you down,
and most of all . . . Faith in Love.

Acknowledgements
XOXOXOXOXOXOXOXO

THERE truly are angels. *How do I know?* Because, this book is in *your* hands. I am so totally taken by the generousity of the many people that appeared to support me and the publication of *I AM Before "I Do."*

This book is dedicated to two groups of people:
First and foremost, to young women *everywhere* who have the power to choose when and whom they marry. May you be brave and not only find a lifetime of love, but may you provide a healthy environment for children if you decide to start a family.

Secondly, to *all of you* who have touched my life while I was finding my "I AM" - (in no specific order & I apologize to anyone I forgot)
Marcie & Paul Judd, Joey & Daria Spina, Tara Estlin, Trish Neal, Wally Hass, Rhoda Grotstein, Rhea Shenin, Diane Gubin, Jeff Harris, Diller Media, Dean Konell, Philip Cheung, David Wavro, Jillian Thomas, Kalene Turnley, Marie Innuso, Raelea Apolito, Suzi Biederman, Louise Urbano, Dr. Mitch Cohen, Rhonda Britten, Linda Sivertsen, Kenneth Schwartz, Lenny Dave, Nick Gorely, Donna Straus, Carol Reisinger, Rami Assouline, Gibby McCaleb, Dana Dotoli, Danielle Detoli, Andrea Fishman, David Katz, Gail Moulton, Jeff Wolf, David Katz, Laurie Chatterton, Joe-Joe Tucci, Dick Clark and The Other Half, Lisa Kazanjian, Cathy Onion, Kelly Raia, Liza Lucas, Dan Poynter, Cary Ginell at Alfred Publishing, Melinda Mondrala at Universal Music Publishing Group, Swork Coffee, CinderellaCakes.com.

* *To the Queen Of Alpha Females - Michele Judd (Shel),*
Thank you for your friendship and loving support from Day One.

** *To my beautiful and dedicated assistant - Julie Vo,*
Thank you for your belief in this project. You are an amazing young woman, and I am so blessed to have you in my life. There is no one else that I would rather have on my team.

"Man is as vast as he acts."

Acknowledgements
XOXOXOXOXOXOXOXOXO

**** A special note to a special man: BLF, thank you for your kindness. You have such a generous heart. What a blessing it was to have shared time with you. As I say in this book, we each must look at what we are saying "I Do" to, and understand that the decision must come half from our heart and half from our head. I know my "I AM." One fine day, I will "I Do."*

To any of the men who have been a part of my life, who believe it is your actions being described on these pages - get over yourselves. I thank you for all the experiences, both good and bad, for they have helped make me what I am today:

A fearless, intelligent, open-eyed, experienced,
confident, loving, and lovable woman.

I give up no apologies for writing this book to the men that grace this earth. Look out guys - women reading this book are going to increase the percentage of fearless, intelligent, open-eyed, experienced, confident, loving, and lovable women out there on the planet. You will have no choice but to rise to the occasion, and I look forward to it, because I can't help myself - I love men.

Angelina & Jake,
May you grow up in a society where
the vow of marriage is preceded by a vow to oneself.
And, may that ever-important step in one's life,
support a world of more healthy & happy families.

May God be very close to you -
May He guide, protect, and bless you
And fill your life with happiness.

Mom,
Thank you for telling me over and over again that there is more to life than boys. Thank you for telling me over and over and over again that I had to make a choice - risk getting pregnant at a young age or having the opportunity to follow my dreams.

I did not always think about the possible consequences of my actions, but I now understand that society's idea of "what is right" is not necessarily a set-up for success in life.

You're the best, Mom! This book is as much yours, as it is mine.

Dad,
Thank you for taking the time during my childhood to show me how to build really cool sand castles. Little did I realize that one day I would have to learn how to create my own castle before Prince Charming is chosen in order to live out the fairytale.

Your castles always blew away all the others, Dad. Build a new one now. I have faith in you.

Gram,
Your prayers helped! The book is finished - I can get married now!

And, the journey continues...

MUSIC LYRIC PERMISSIONS

"I Would've Loved You Anyway" by Troy Vargas
Copyright 2001 by Songs of Universal
All rights administered by Songs of Universal / BMI
Used by Permission. All Rights Reserved.

I Would've Loved You Anyway
Words and Music by Mary Danna and Troy Vargas
Copyright 2001 by Ensign Music Corporation, Danna Songs and Songs of Universal, Inc.
International Copyright Secured All Rights Reserved

"I Hope You Dance" by Mark D. Sanders
Copyright 2000 by MCA Music Publishing, Soda Creek Songs
All rights administered by Universal Music Corp. / ASCAP
Used by Permission. All Rights Reserved.

I Hope You Dance
Words and Music by Tia Sillers and Mark D. Sanders
Copyright 2000 by Choice is Tragic Music, Ensign Music Corporation, Universal Music Corp. and Soda Creek Songs
All Rights for Soda Creek Songs Controlled and Administered by Universal Music Corp.
International Copyright Secured All Rights Reserved

"Look Heart, No Hands" by Howard Russell Smith, Trey Edwin Bruce
Copyright 1992 by MCA Publishing, Love My Music
All rights administered by Universal Music Corp. / ASCAP
Used by Permission. All Rights Reserved.

"Love Will Find a Way" by Cory Charles Lerios, David Michael Jenkins
Copyright 1978 by Almo Music Corp., Pablo Cruise Music
All rights administered by Almo Music Corp. / ASCAP
Used by Permission. All Rights Reserved.

"Shut Up and Drive" by Melvern Rivers Rutherford II
Copyright 1997 by Music Corporation of America
All rights administered by Songs of Universal, Inc. / BMI
Used by Permission. All Rights Reserved.

"SHUT UP AND DRIVE"
Composers: Sam Tate - Annie Tate - Rivers Rutherford
Copyright 1997. Critter City Music (SESAC)
Administered by Bluewater Music Services Corp.
Used by Permission.

"I'm Gonna Wash That Man Right Outa My Hair"
by Richard Rodgers and Oscar Hammerstein II
Copyright 1949 by Richard Rodgers Oscar Hammerstein II
Copyright Renewed
WILLIAMSON MUSIC owner of publication and allied rights throughout the World
International Copyright Secured All Rights Reserved Used by Permission

Better Than Nothing
from The Braxton Brothers' CD, "Both Sides"
Written by Wayne Braxton, Sundra Manning
(Braxton Brothers Productions/ASCAP, Nafasi Songs/ASCAP, LeSun Music/ASCAP)
(Contains sample of *Remind Me* by Patrice Rushen and Karen Evans
published by Baby Fingers Music/ASCAP)

MUSIC LYRIC PERMISSIONS

HOLD ME
Words and Music by DARREN HAYES and DANIEL JONES
Copyright 1999 ROUGH CUT MUSIC PTY. LTD.
All Rights in the U.S. and Canada Administered by WB MUSIC CORP.
All Rights Reserved Used by Permission

IN THE STILL OF THE NIGHT
Words and Music by COLE PORTER
Copyright 1937 (Renewed) CHAPPELL & CO.
All Rights Reserved Used by Permission

LOVE LIFT ME
Words and Music by ERIC BAZILIAN, JOHN BETTIS, RANDY CANTOR, AND AMANDA MARSHALL
Copyright 1999 HUMAN BOY MUSIC, JOHN BETTIS MUSIC, RANDY MICHELLE MUSIC, AND METATUNE INC.
All Rights for HUMAN BOY MUSIC and JOHN BETTIS MUSIC Administered by WB MUSIC CORP.
All Rights Reserved Used by Permission

LOVE YOU INSIDE AND OUT
Words and music by BARRY GIBB, MAURICE GIBB, and ROBIN GIBB
Copyright 1979 CROMPTON SONGS LLC
Administered by WARNER-TAMERLANE PUBLISHING CORP.
All Rights Reserved Used by Permission

(YOUR LOVE HAS LIFTED ME) HIGHER AND HIGHER
Words and Music by GARY JACKSON, CARL SMITH AND RAYNARD MINER
Copyright 1967 (Renewed) CHEVIS MUSIC, INC., WARNER-TAMERLANE PUBLISHING CORP. and UNICHAPPELL MUSIC INC.
All Rights Reserved Used by Permission

WHY DON'T YOU AND I
Words and Music by CHAD KROEGER
Copyright 2002 ANAESTHETIC MUSIC and WARNER-TAMERLANE PUBLISHING CORP.
All Rights Administered by WARNER-TAMERLANE PUBLISHING CORP.
All Rights Reserved Used by Permission

LOVE WALKS IN
Words and Music by EDWARD VAN HALEN, SAMMY HAGAR, ALEX VAN HALEN, MICHAEL ANTHONY
Copyright 1986 WB MUSIC CORP. and YESSUP MUSIC COMPANY
All Rights Administered by WB MUSIC CORP.
All Rights Reserved Used by Permission

MY OWN BEST FRIEND
Words and music by JOHN KANDER and FRED EBB
Copyright 1973 (Renewed) UNICHAPPELL MUSIC INC. and KANDER & EBB, INC.
All Rights Reserved Used by Permission

Cover & Bio Photography
Zarek Dietz
www.photographybyzarek.com

Ranee's Hair Stylist
Elisa Loretta Perez
www.elisasgarage.com

Cover Model
Vince Adams

Wedding Dress Courtesy of
Michelle Ventresca

Please visit
www.iambeforeido.com
for release dates of:

Loving Out Loud On Campus -
Volume One & Two on DVD
Ranee on location interviewing students
about relationships

TOP 100 Questions
Asked by College
Students Today
A Dating, Love, Sex, & Marriage Q&A

Why Cinderella Gets Divorced
and Goldilocks Doesn't
A real life tale about
modern love

What She Wants
to Hear
Lyrics that convey what women
long to hear from their man

We all know at least three women who could benefit from reading this book.

Tell them about it, email them about it, or buy it as a gift for them!